THE VOICE OF MAN

BY NICK MERRILL

QUOCUNQUE JECERIS STABIT

Lulu Books

Morrisville, North Carolina

THE VOICE OF MAN

Copyright © 2008 by Nick Merrill
Cover photo by Braydie Grove
Book design by Nick Merrill

ISBN: 978-0-578-01235-3

For Brian and Adrian,
For the Island's children, past, present and future.
For everyone who told me I could,
For everyone who told me I couldn't,
And, above all, for Mom and Dad.

ONE

The plane's two propellers changed pitch, stirring me gently awake. I opened my raw, jet-lagged eyes and, blinded by the sterile white of the plane's interior, clenched them shut again and collapsed backwards into my seat. After sixteen hours of customs lines, luggage searches, international terminals at unfamiliar airports, suspicious glances ("You're going *where*, exactly?"), shaky takeoffs, and turbulent flights, I was suspended thousands of feet above the Irish Sea aboard a sputtering propeller plane. I began to wonder how I'd gotten myself in such a predicament.

In the midst of the scattered confusion that surrounded my junior year of high school, I heard about a Fellowship opportunity. Essentially, students were to write a proposal for a project (any project at all!) and the proposition deemed most worthy would be funded in full by the headmaster himself.

I began researching endangered languages. I had a burning curiosity about languages and, fueled by childhood memories of Indiana Jones movies, I imagined myself traveling to a distant corner of the earth and shining a light on an obscure subject.

I soon stumbled upon a list of endangered languages. I was looking for a language with a critically small number of speakers (preferably one that had yet to be thoroughly documented). A few pages into the list, something caught my eye.

Manx, a language from the Isle of Man, had only fifty-four fluent speakers and sparse literature.

I had never heard of the Isle of Man. In fact, I doubted it was a real place until I got my hands on an atlas. I was surprised to note its location: a conspicuous dot between England and Ireland. I suppose my eye had skipped over it during my sixteen years of looking at world maps. And I suppose the adults teaching me geography failed to mention it even when discussing European political boundaries in the most excruciating detail.

The Isle of Man, called simply "The Island" by its locals, is a self-governing Crown dependency, home of the oldest currently functioning parliament in the world (founded in 979 AD) and the center of Europe's offshore banking industry (the Island is one of HSBC's main European hubs).

The rest of the application process is a blur. I remember writing a three or four page report detailing why saving a language is worth a large sum of money, and why Manx is a language worth saving. I remember sending it to my dean attached to an email that said, "I think I might be insane, but could you take a look at this?" I remember getting a note in the middle of a test months later that read, "Please report to the headmaster's office after school."

I remember sprinting up the spiral staircase of the school's tower, racing through the wooded alcove that separates Mr. Hudnut's office from the rest of the school, and sitting down in front of an imposing desk and a bookcase stacked with an intimidating number of leather-bound tomes. I remember Mr. Hudnut shaking my hand and telling me, "You're going to the Isle of Man."

I opened my eyes again, this time cautiously. Two of the other passengers on the plane were asleep, and the third was staring blankly at the back of the seat in front of her.

I slid the plastic curtain away from my window to reveal a rocky mass—an island shadowed against the dark sea, an ancient land with an ancient tongue that had only fifty-four speakers, and I had traveled halfway around the world to become the fifty-fifth.

Two

Many people are taken aback when they hear that Manx is "endangered," as they interpret it to mean that the Manx people are on their way to extinction. It is a common misconception that language death is related to the death of actual people. In reality, the population of the Isle of Man has been increasing steadily over the past one hundred years (and has enjoyed quite a boost in population growth over the past twenty years due to immigration from the UK).

Language death is related only to the number of persons who speak a language natively. In almost all cases, a language dies when a population becomes bilingual and gradually shifts its preference from one language to another, usually over the course of hundreds of years. Specifically, when native speakers stop teaching a language to their children, a language is deemed "moribund" and it begins to fade away. Such has been the case on the Island.

At face value, it may seem bizarre to claim that entire groups of people begin to prefer speaking a new language to the one traditionally spoken by their ancestors. What could possibly cause such a drastic shift to occur?

The obvious culprits are massive immigration, forced exodus, and genocide. Although these have caused many of history's most notable language extinctions (Hebrew being the most well-known), none of these reasons had a hand in Manx's decline. One would imagine that language extinction is rare, reserved for catastrophic events. For almost four thousand years of human existence, this was true.

Linguists Michael Krauss and Steven Wurm have estimated that almost 3,000 of the world's 7,000 languages will vanish by 2100. In our increasingly interconnected age, learning a "universal" language such as English has become a necessity for speakers of minority languages, and many of these languages are hurtling toward extinction at an alarming rate. The Grimes Ethnolauge notes that 52% of the world's languages are spoken by less than 10,000 people, and 83% are confined to a single country. In fact, 50% of the world's population speaks one of ten languages; Krauss and Wurm's estimate seems conservative in light of this and, indeed, many linguists estimate that only 1,500 languages may remain by the end of the 21st century.

One such language is Manx: limited to the Isle of Man, Manx is currently spoken by only fifty-four individuals. This figure is derived from the number of students and instructors at the Manx Language School at the Island of Man College, all of whom are classified as native speakers, as they have been speaking Manx since childhood. No other native speakers have been documented. All of the Island's 80,000 inhabitants speak British English, and few remnants of the Island's Manx past remain.

Why, then, would one save an endangered language? Lack of linguistic diversity may seem beneficial: a decrease in world languages could facilitate better global communication and could perhaps create a more peaceful world community.

As the famous (or, to some, infamous) linguist Noam Chomsky once said: "Language is the DNA of culture." Indeed, the roots of a single word can reveal volumes about the origins of an entire group of persons: for example, the Manx word for "horse," *cabbyl,* is directly related to the Vulgar Latin word *caballus,* also meaning horse. Although some anthropologists have suggested that Gaelic languages such as Manx were untouched by Romantic influence, the single Manx word *cabbyl* brings this theory crumbling to the ground. Clearly, without linguistic clues, studying a culture devolves into guesswork. Even when a dead language has a rich literature, without auditory cues we are left with a less than complete understanding of the culture that language describes (imagine if modern humans knew what Classical Latin sounded like!). Ultimately, although a particular ethnic group may be unaffected by the extinction of its language, the loss will always leave humanity poorer.

Of course, the fact remains that the world is undergoing a dramatic shift. In many ways, our world is getting smaller as technology ties us more closely to our fellow humans. In this age, agreeing on common languages is not simply convenient but in many cases essential to progress, so it is understandable that speakers of smaller languages with little influence on the global stage are beginning to prefer larger, more global languages to their traditional tongues.

It would be ridiculous to attempt to stem the profound technological and social forces that are causing the loss of language. My aim on the Island was not to encourage Manx speakers to teach their children Manx, or to "sell" Manx to a new audience. I had two goals for my project: primarily, I intended to thoroughly document and record Manx while finding all literature I could on or in the language; secondarily, I hoped to understand the Isle of Man as an example of the larger phenomenon of global linguistic convergence.

I entered the fellowship mostly with questions. What *exactly* caused Manx to go extinct? What *exactly* led to its revival? Can the history of the Manx language be related to those of other languages that have taken similar paths?

And there was, of course, my most important question: can we learn enough from Manx's story to save the hundreds of languages threatened with complete extinction?

THREE

The brakes locked and the plane skidded to a halt on the short runway (made considerably shorter by an archaeological dig at the airstrip's end). I stumbled off the plane bleary-eyed and foggy, dragging my feet across the runway toward a sliding glass door. Halfway across the runway, something in my sleepless brain told me to stop.

It was early morning. The world was blue-gray and dimmed softly like a film noir movie. An attendant on the runway, his silver hair glowing in the early light, glanced at me, his blue eyes alight with a mix suspicion and weariness. His eyes flickered away.

I looked to my left. A stone clock tower rose above castle walls only a few hundred feet in the distance. The castle was surrounded by open fields and gentle, rolling hills. The face of the clock tower was blue, corroded by age. I felt a tinge of recognition. A chill wind whistled through the trees, whipping across my face.

Hailing a taxi was more difficult than I would have anticipated. After carefully observing the three other passengers' taxi-waving technique, a gruff, bearded driver pulled up in front of me. I rushed into his cab.

"Where you off to?" he asked.

"King William's college."

The driver turned around, "King Bill's? Are ya really now?" I assumed I had managed to offend someone already. "You could just walk there, you know?" I *knew* that clock tower looked familiar: I had seen a few pictures of King William's college, one of which featured the tower prominently. "Well, good enough. I won't charge ya. Ya ain't from around here I reckon."

King William's College was founded in 1668, named after King William IV who, when asked for a contribution, said "I offer my most valuable possession: my name." The campus, which normally houses 500 students, ages 3 to 18, lies on the coast of Castletown and stretches across acres of pristinely kept cricket greens. The students were off for the summer, and I was allowed to stay in one of the campus's houses with a few archaeology students from the University of Liverpool who were excavating an ancient Abby near Castletown and assisting around the grounds of Castle Rushen, a meticulously maintained Castle for which the town (*Balley Chashtal* Manx) is named.

"So, American or Canadian?"

"Oh, American."

"Are ya? I can never tell the difference. Is there a difference?"

"There's a difference, yeah."

"I can tell it when you folk talk all drawling like the president but I can never tell with the other folk, yessir." He stopped the taxi in front of the clock tower, the cricket greens rolling into the sea to the East. Before I could thank the driver for the free ride, he zipped off into the road, leaving a trail of dust and fumes in his wake. I was starting to get a headache from exhaustion, and the smell of gasoline certainly didn't help.

I walked into the Junior House, a two-story dormitory complex that seemed to have enjoyed few renovations since its construction in the early 20th century. The caretaker, Max, greeted me. A short fellow with receding red hair, Max welcomed me warmly and segued masterfully into a twenty-minute lecture on motor sports, occasionally interrupted by sparse descriptions of the house's facilities.

"The motorbikes race around Castle Rushen and—this is the laundry room, you see—yes, they go almost a hundred kilometers an hour, they do, and they come right round the harbor almost on their sides they're going so fast, you know—this is my room if you need me—there's a race just tonight, there is."

By the time Max led me into my room, my head felt as if it were about to split in half. It was a relatively spacious studio: a three-person, ground-floor room with a view of the Irish Sea, then painted red against the rising sun.

"The Liverpool students are out digging already," Max told me. "Nice and early to beat the heat, you know. So you won't meet your roommates until later. In the meantime... Well, you look tired, mate. Don't blame ya, what coming from America and all. It's four in the mornin', anyway. Maybe some rest would do you good."

"Yeah, rest sounds nice, actually." Max shuffled out, shutting the door behind him. Immediately, I threw myself headlong onto my bed and collapsed into sleep.

FOUR

The hard historical evidence of the Isle of Man's history is sparse and filled generously with mythology to compensate. According to the myth, the bearded wizard Manannán lived alone in a Castle on the Island. He would envelop the Island in a thick mist to deter invaders, keeping the prehistoric Manx people sheltered from the outside world. Manannán's name is widely believed to have led to the Manx *Ellan Vannin,* meaning "Man's Isle," from which the modern name "Isle of Man" is derived.

As far as actual evidence goes, the Manx Museum holds artifacts from as early as the Mesolithic Period (about 11,500 to 5000 BCE), mostly tools made of flint or bone. Some tools have been recovered from the Neolithic Period (about 5000 to 2500 BCE) as well.

Manx's story begins, however, in the Iron Age. Along with forts and other military structures, the Iron Age (starting in about 800 BCE) saw the appearance of curious stones about the Island. These stones, called Ogham stones, are normally flat with a series of puzzling (though obviously intentional) scratch marks. Around four hundred of these stones have been recovered across Ireland and Britain, and the scratch marks (which assign names of trees to individual letters) compose the sounds of various Celtic languages. Around 700 BCE, the Ogham inscriptions underwent a shift. The Ogham stones that date from before 700 BCE on the island featured Brythonic-language inscriptions (the family of languages that originated in modern day England and Wales); Ogham stones from after 700 BCE, however, contain Goidelic-language inscriptions (the language family that originated in modern day Ireland). This shift in the preferred inscription language on the Island points to an influx of Celts (due either to invasion or immigration) and, since modern Manx belongs to the Goidelic family, we may assume that these Goidelic-language-speaking Celts assimilated with the indigenous Brythonic-language speakers, creating the basis for the modern Manx language.

Between approximately 800 and 850 AD, Vikings (or "Northmen," as the early Manx texts describe them) visited the Island searching primarily for wealth. The Vikings returned to the Island between 850 and 1000AD, placing the the Isle firmly under Scandinavian rule and transforming it into a permanent base of operations: the legendary Norse conqueror Godred Crovan created and ruled the Kingdom of Man and the Isles, a monarchy ruling over British Isles with St Patrick's Isle (a small island off the coast of the Isle of Man) as its capital. It is during this period that Manx gained its

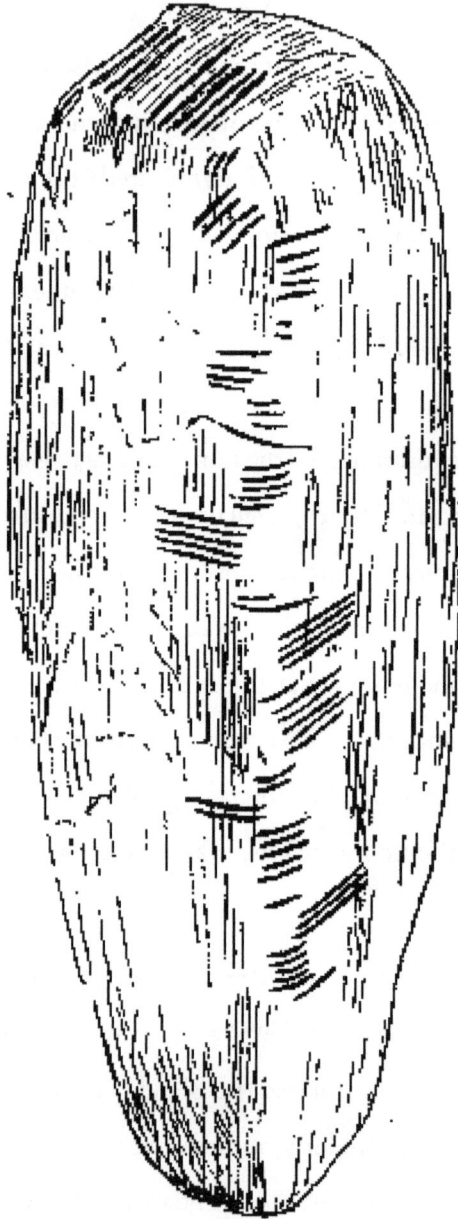

An Ogham Stone. Kermode, P. M. C. (1911) <u>The Manx Archaeological Survey</u>. 3rd Report. Douglas.

most distinctive feature: Scandinavian influence. Although Manx is certainly a Goidelic tongue, it is the only Celtic language to feature a significant amount of Scandinavian-derived vocabulary (in fact, Manx borrowed a few names directly from Viking languages, such as *Asmund*, *Biorn*, *Thorstein*, and even the name *Viking*). The Vikings also contributed the word *tynwald,* meaning "meeting place," to the Manx language. Tynwald is the name of the modern Manx parliament, and the ancient mound upon which the elders originally met is still used today during the Manx holiday of Tynwald Day, July 5th.

The remainder of the Vikings' reign on the Island was relatively uneventful. Godred's son, Olaf (reigned 1113 – 1152) allied so closely with the Irish and Scottish kings that no one dared to challenge his rule. By the middle of the 13th century, however, Norway began to lose its political dominance to Scotland. In 1266, King Magnus IV of Norway sold the Island to Scotland for 4,000 merks along with a 100-merk annuity.

The crumbling foreign rule that plagued the Island had finally given way to a relatively peaceful Scottish rule. Beginning in 1290, however, a period of political instability eventually resulted in Anglo control of the Island.

The period of Manx history between 1290 and 1430 seems more like a fanciful story than like actual history. King Edward I took control of the Island from the Scottish, possessing it until the Scottish hero Robert Bruce took the Island almost singlehandedly after a five-week siege upon Castle Rushen. The Island remained under Scottish rule until 1346, when England won the legendary Battle of Neville's Cross in which 3,000 English soldiers defeated 12,000 Scottish (the Scottish suffered 7,000 casualties while the English lost only 100 men). In 1333, King Edward III granted absolute power over the Isle of Man to the English nobleman William de Montecute. About sixty years later, Richard le Scrope, a supporter of Richard II's rule, bought the Isle of Man from Montecute's son as an extravagant gift for his favorite son, William. After usurping Richard II, King Henry IV, outraged that the Island was under the control of a political dissident, beheaded le Scrope (in public, of course) and put the Isle of Man under direct British rule in 1399. The rule lasted until 1406, when Henry IV granted the Island to Sir John Stanley and his heirs under the condition that the Stanley family present two falcons to all future Kings and Queens of England upon their coronations. Yes, falcons. Two of them.

It is important to note that the Manx people had no say in their own political destiny during this period. Their ancestral home had been passed from hand to hand for more than four centuries, rarely remaining under a single ruler for more than a few years. The Manx did, however, maintain Tynwald. The parliament has been in continuous existence since its conception in 979, and though its powers were certainly limited during periods of foreign rule, the assembly met at least once per year from its conception until today.

A few rebellions took place after the British Crown secured its power, the most notable of which was the Manxman Illiam Dhone's rebellion. Dhone managed to capture all castles and forts on the Island in October, 1651, and remained Governor of the Isle of Man until he was executed at gunpoint in 1663 for "misappropriated funds." Despite

Dhone's brief rule and a few other periods of minor tension between Man and Great Britain, the English Crown maintained long-term control over the Island.

At this point, Manx existed more or less in its modern form; all of Manx's foreign influences had played their parts in forming the language. A 1780 Manx grammar written by John Kelly, an English reverend, details a Manx language almost identical to the one spoken today.

A unique Manx language had been forged over seven hundred years of political twists and turns and, almost immediately, a British imperial power began to threaten this new tongue.

A PRACTICAL GRAMMAR

OF THE

ANTIENT GAELIC,

OR

Language of the Isle of Man,

USUALLY CALLED

MANKS.

BY THE REV. JOHN KELLY, LL.D.,

VICAR OF ARDLEIGH, AND RECTOR OF COPFORD,
IN THE COUNTY OF ESSEX.

EDITED, TOGETHER

WITH AN INTRODUCTION, LIFE OF DR. KELLY, AND NOTES,

BY THE

REV. WILLIAM GILL,

VICAR OF MALEW.

DOUGLAS, ISLE OF MAN:
PRINTED FOR THE MANX SOCIETY.
MDCCCLIX.

FACSIMILE REPRINT FOR BERNARD QUARITCH, 15 PICCADILLY, LONDON.
1870.

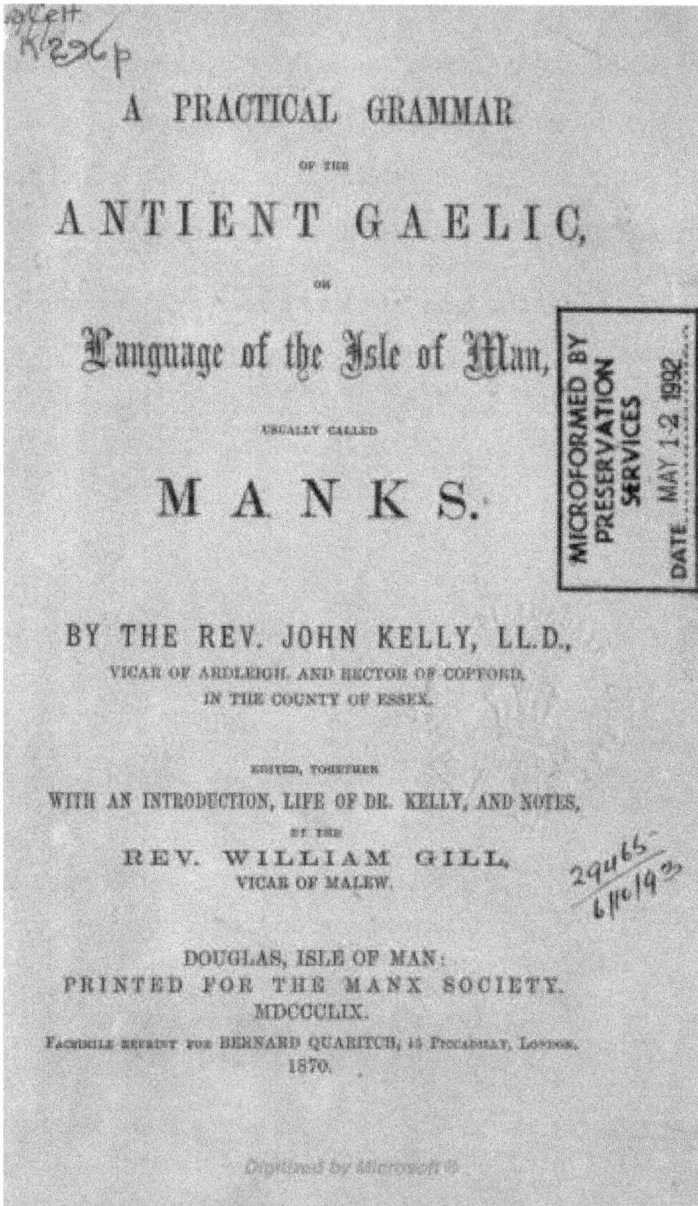

Reverend Kelly's *Manx Grammar*.

FIVE

I was walking down San Vicente Blvd. in Los Angeles. It was a balmy night, and cars whizzed by me, their headlights dashing bright whites across the sidewalk. I passed a trendy sushi restaurant brimming with customers.

Suddenly, an imposing bell sounded from inside. The chatter from the shop continued to flow out onto the street. I peered curiously into the shop. The crisply dressed men laughed slyly, and the ladies were decked head to toe in LA's freshest and trendiest. I was sporting a T-shirt and jeans; clearly, the restaurant was no place for me.

The bell chimed again, resonating deeply from inside the shop. The diners chatted on, seemingly unaware of the ominous sound that echoed around them. A third chime. I walked in, staring curiously at the chic faces, the expensive sunglasses, the polished chopsticks, the freshly pressed sport jackets. A fourth chime echoed from the bar at the back of the shop, drowning out the excited chatter around the diners.

My eyes shot open. A fifth chime, a sixth chime, a seventh, an eighth, a ninth.

I stared at the cracking plaster on the ceiling. The bed was springy and unpleasant. It was still a few hours before I would have liked to be awake, and I had yet to meet my roommates, who were scheduled to come home at three. Regardless, I had work to do.

I had exchanged a few emails with an advocate of Manx education named Adrian Cain, and Adrian advised that I speak with a man named Brian Stowell immediately upon my arrival.

I found Brian's name quickly enough in the phonebook, and I waited until 9:30 to give him a ring. Courtesy, I figured. After a few rings, a spry voice answered.

"Hello?"

"Hi, my name's Nick Merrill, and I'm visiting from the US to research Manx. I've been told that—"

"Oh, you're the visitor! Yes yes, Adrian's told me about you. Well, I suppose you want to interview me, then?"

"Well—yes, that would be great, actually. Are you free around two today?"

"Yes, two would be lovely. I'll meet you for tea at my home in Douglas. It's at 18 Hillary Road—just ask around when you arrive in town and they'll point you in the right direction." I scribbled the address down in my notebook. I threw on a jacket and packed my briefcase: a notebook, a few pens, a tape recorder, three tapes, extra batteries, and a camera. Tools of the trade, I suppose.

I trotted briskly out the door. The sun was up now, though it had yet to make its way through the clouds, and the early day had an impolite briskness to it. I made my way to the bus stop across the street from the campus grounds, and shivered quietly under my jacket as I awaited the 9:45 bus bound for Douglas.

A twenty-minute double-decker bus ride took me to the center of a steeply slanted road, lined high with office buildings. Logos of haughtily named financial firms populated the town, interjected sparsely with craft shops and bakeries. The city seemed to slide from green-specked cliffs down into the Irish Sea below, and a few dozen people (a relatively large number given the population density around Castletown) scurried busily across the streets.

Three and a half hours of exploring later, it was time to find Brian's house. An elderly lady pointed me up the main promenade and directed me to turn right at the Freemasonry Lodge ("You won't miss it, I promise," she told me).

The overcast sky had just begun to rain as I made my way to 18 Hillary Road. It was a modest home with a slate roof and a white picket

King William's Clocktower at early morning.

fence. I spent about thirty seconds looking for the doorbell before I realized that I was searching in vain. I pulled my jacket above my head and knocked.

The door opened to reveal an elderly man in a wool sweater. He had twinkling blue eyes, contrasted sharply against a thick layer of gray hair and a scruff, white beard.

"Ah, you're just on time! Yes, come in." The man ushered me in, closing the door behind me. "Dreadful weather today, isn't it? Well, have a seat in my study."

Brian's study was a cozy room, overflowing with books: papers lay scattered across every flat surface in the room, and volumes of books seemed to explode from overly packed shelves. I introduced myself formally, asked if I could record our conversation and, upon Brian's approval, I flipped on my tape recorder and placed it on Brian's desk.

Brian poured two cups of tea across the room. The smell of a burning fireplace lingered in the air. The rain beat gently on the pavement outside, and the tape recorder emitted a faint hiss from the table.

"Well, do begin, young man," he said.

I hadn't ever conducted an interview before. My father was a journalist, and he imparted a few pieces of advice to me before I left. I read a bit about conducting a proper interview. I just hadn't *actually* conducted one.

I can sense my nerves when I listen to the tape today. There's the shuffle of my jacket as I shift in my seat. There's the clink of Brian's teacup against the china coaster. There's the rustling of pages as I tried to remember where in my notebook I had written down my questions. I had

written a series of (what I thought were) poignant questions about Manx,

Brian's involvement in the language and its revival, his journey in learning

the language, and even about his work as a physicist when he was younger.

"How did you get involved in Manx?" A standard first question, as I

understood. I was told to expect a brief answer as the interviewee warmed

up.

Listening to that tape today, I can hear Brian's coaster skid across

the table. "Well, I suppose I might as well begin by telling you everything

and you can just ask about whatever I've left out. How does that sound?"

Brian Stowell in his study.

SIX

When Rev. John Kelly published his <u>Practical Grammar</u> in 1780, Manx was by far the majority language of the Island. In fact, Kelly wrote the book to aid missionaries from England who wished to perform religious work on the Island.

Almost seventy years later, Englishman J.G. Cumming wrote in his <u>Account of the Isle of Man</u> (1848), "there are ... few persons (perhaps none of the young) who speak no English."

In 1874, Celtic Scholar Henry Jenner estimated that only 30% of the population spoke Manx regularly. By 1901, the Census revealed that a meager 9.1% of Manx citizens spoke Manx. By 1921, only 1.1% spoke the language.

The decline in spoken Manx was sudden and significant. In only a century and a half, Manx declined from a majority language to a status of extreme endangerment, having well under 1,000 speakers by the 1921 census. So, what happened?

One answer comes from English politician James Chaloner, who wrote a few notes on the Manx language in his <u>Short Treatise on the Isle of Man</u> (c. 1640).

"It is worth the observing, that many of their words are derived from the Latine and Greek, and some are of pure English; such words, for the most part, signifie things Forraign, and which originally were not known to them, or in use amongst them...

"It is more then probable that as their speech first (as of all other Nations) consisted of few, but significant words suitable to the simplicity of their Manners; so, in processe of time, by their conversation with Strangers, alteration of manners, Forraign Merchandize and new Inventions came to be introduced, which necessitated them to an enlargment of their speech: But finding it more easie to take the words of such by whom they were introduced, then to coyn new of their own, these Mixtures of Languages have in all likelyhood been produced."

Though primitive, Chaloner's analysis is essentially accurate: even by 1868, British economic and cultural influence on the Island had altered the language's lexicon significantly. A fairly typical loanword relationship developed: with an influx of English technology and culture, Manx people needed words to describe the new injections into their universe and, since borrowing is easier than inventing, Manx people used more and more English to describe the world around them.

Although Chaloner's words predated Manx's decline by a few hundred years, his point proved central to Manx's eventual extinction. The Manx poet TE Brown (1830-1897) was educated at King William's College. A contemporary of J.G. Cumming. Brown wrote in the language that most Manx people of the time spoke.

> *"Yiss ! yiss ! muss hev a kiss'*
>
> *Aw, Kitty, Kitty bogh !*
>
> *Aw my gough!*
>
> *Kitty darlin' ! Kitty then!*
>
> *And me so far away!"*

Though the excerpt from the above poem, *The Christening*, does contain some Manx features (*bogh*, here meaning "boy," *gough,* here meaning girl) and some interesting phonology ("yiss" in place of "yes," "hev" in place of "have"), the passage is obviously not written in Manx; as Brown's poem demonstrates, the mid 19th century saw an almost complete displacement of Manx in favor of English due to a tradition of language sharing that (as Chaloner's remarks would indicate) dated back to at least the mid 1600s.

J.G. Cummings republished Chaloner's work in 1863. He made an astonishingly accurate prediction in a comment on Chaloner's Treatise. Chaloner wrote of the Manx people, "Few speak the English Tongue," to which Cummings appended:

... for mine own people do I sing,
And use the old familiar speech:
Happy if I shall reach
Their inmost consciousness.

TE Brown's poetry (a verse referencing the unique dialect of English spoken in on the Island during the 19th century) adorns the walls of the Manx Heritage Museum in Douglas.

"In a few years it may perhaps be written, "Few speak the Manx Tongue." It is a doomed language— an iceberg floating in southern latitudes."... It is much to be hoped that... philologists of future ages, may have within easy reach the means of investigating and comparing the extinct languages of the British Isles."

Cummings's prophecy came true. By the 1930s, only a few elderly Manxman spoke any Manx. Parents were not teaching their children Manx, and British influence had created an Island robbed of its traditional language.

In 1936, it was onto this Island that Brian Stowell was born.

During Brian's childhood, few adults mentioned the Manx language. When they did, it was often in joking, making snide references to a barbaric past. Some adults had a vehement, often aggressive distaste for Manx.

"I recall that one could start a fight speaking Manx," Brian mused. "A group of fellows walked into a pub once and greeted the bartender in Manx—this was about 1950, I'd say—and one gentleman up and yelled at them! 'How dare you march in here and speak like that! Manx was never a proper language!' That's what they'd all say: 'Manx was never a proper language.' When I was a teenager, my church conducted [a service] from the Manx bible one day just for laughs—all in good humor, you know—and an older man got so worked up yelling about Manx he had to sit down for fear of fainting."

I asked Brian if he had any idea why older Manxmen regarded the language in this way.

"It was a sign of poverty, really... No one of any authority or standing spoke Manx. It would be quite unbecoming for a businessman to speak Manx, and he'd have to speak in English to the British clients, after all."

The adults' bizarre attitude toward Manx intrigued the teenage Brian. In 1963, Brian was introduced to Ned Maddrell, an older Manx speaker. "He seemed to be lamenting the fact that nobody was interested in Manx," Brian recalls. "A fellow called Burny Cain was still around... I went round with him and Doug and picked the language up."

Brian learned from the authentic sources, to be sure. Although Brian was not raised on the language (and since he was a young adult when he learned Manx, he can't be regarded as a true native speaker), he was fluent in the language within a few years.

Brian, along with Burny and Doug, swept across the Island, making vinyl recordings of the last living native speakers of the Manx language, ultimately collecting over an hour of native speech.

Stowell left the Island for England and spent the following decades of his life working as a physicist in the Atomic Energy Department of the British government (Brian wrote his notes in Manx to preserve the secrecy of his projects). After about twenty years of service to Her Majesty's Government, he returned to 18 Hillary Road to devote himself to Manx education.

The older people of his generation were gone, then; he was now a member of the "older class," and the fellow members of his generation knew little about Manx besides the fact that it was completely extinct.

He started Manx classes out of his home. The classes attracted very little attention: two or three people at most would express interest in learning the Island's native tongue. His students would meet for tea and throw around casual conversation, mostly shooting the breeze to practice Manx conversational skills. This continued on throughout the 80s and 90s.

Then, one day in 1996, fifteen people showed up at his door wanting to learn Manx. The next day, ten more. He went directly to the local high school to convince the board to allow him to teach Manx as an elective class. The board, assuming that few children would actually sign up, agreed to the proposition.

"They assumed it would be like a cello or a violin class. You take a class of children and ask them who'd like to learn the flute, and you get one or two hands. So the principal went to the students and asked them, 'Who'd like to learn Manx?' Only two students *didn't* want to take a class in the language. You should have seen the look on the principal's face!"

Soon thereafter, the entire Island buzzed with excitement. "Adults who had never heard a word of Manx in their life greeted one another with typical Manx greetings," Brian told me.

Manx went from being spoken by 100% of the Island in the 1700s to 1% in the 1920s, and practically died completely during the middle of the 20th century. Then, in the late 20th century, a seemingly magic revival occurred during which the formerly bitter attitude toward Manx seemed to be erased completely.

Why? What happened to cause this change? If British influence caused Manx to decline, then what is responsible for its resurgence on an entirely English-speaking island?

The plot was thickening.

SEVEN

"And the children loved the Manx class, you know—" Brian stopped as the tape recorder clicked off on the table. I rushed to switch the tape out. "Oh, don't bother. I don't have anything else to say, anyway."

I thanked him profusely for the interview. I took a quick glance outside as I put my coat on. "Oh, you aren't planning to walk back to King William's in that weather, are you? Here, let me drive you. I insist."

We sped down the country road in a yellow Peugeot as the rain punished Brian's windshield.

"Thanks so much for driving me back. I just flew in this morning, so I can't quite find my way around."

"Ah, some day this is. The weather's usually much better, you know." Brian's gaze drifted off into the distance. "Oh, I'd almost forgotten!" Brian turned to me with an excited smile. "Adrian is having a Manx study group tonight. Mad Dog's Pub in Port St. Mary. That's *Purt le Moirrey* in Manx, for your information. Eight o' clock tonight. They throw Manx around, but perhaps it will help you pick some up."

"Oh, that sounds great!" My mind began to race as I imagined hearing Manx spoken aloud for the first time. And I'd hear it from none other than Adrian Cain, one of the leading experts on the language.

Brian gave me a few short directions on which bus to take to Port St. Mary as we pulled into King William's. The cricket greens were soaked, and the stone seemed to drip off the clock tower. The slate roof of Junior House appeared metallic in the overcast sky.

I pulled my jacket over my head and stepped out of the car. "Thanks again for the ride!" I yelled to Brian over beating rain.

"Yes, of course, of course. We'll speak soon," he replied.

I turned and walked away, attempting futilely to shield myself from the downpour. I heard a voice behind me.

"Oh, Nick?" Brian called.

"Yeah?"

"So rude of me not to have asked before, but—are you American or Canadian?"

* * *

In Los Angeles, the night descends slowly. In the hours after the sun sets, the night fights off the electric day created by the city lights. I could wander for hours without finding an unlit street.

When the sun sets on the Island, the night crashes down. I couldn't see my hands in front of my face as I walked along the street toward Mad Dog's pub. A few streetlights projected spots of yellow across the pavement. I felt a light drizzle and a bitter cold as I made my way toward an old pub with water-stained walls, its windows illuminated in the foggy night. A single incandescent bulb lit a sign: a picture of a St. Bernard, its eyes wide and red, tongue dangling out to one side:

"MAD DOG'S PUBLIC HOUSE. Open everyday but Sunday. Beer garden from 7 to 10."

The pub's inside held a roar of voices, a pleasant, high-spirited bustle that seemed to reverberate throughout the space. Over the excited tones of the chatter, my ear caught a few peculiar sounds. A rolled "r." A throaty "ch." I searched around for the source of the sound. My eye settled on a thirty-something man with buzzed brown hair, a can of Coke in his hand, chatting excitedly as his mouth moved into foreign shapes. He sat in a booth in the back corner, obscured by the loud English chatter around him.

I walked over, and cocked my head nervously as I looked at the man.

"Hi, sorry, but, are you Adrian Cain?"

I felt an immediate rush of regret. What made me presume that Adrian was that particular man? There was another, older man sitting at the table. I had no idea how old Adrian was. What if I were, in fact, mistaken, and the actual Adrian became offended that I presumed incorrectly.

"Yes yes, that's me! You must be Nick. Come, have a seat, then." Adrian darted up, smiling broadly. He turned to the others seated in the booth: a young woman, cheery looking with red hair tied up in a bun; an older woman, serene and reserved; a middle-aged man, long-faced and solemn, clutching a pint of beer. *"Shoh my charrey Nick. T'eh cummal anys Los Angeles, as t'eh ynsaghey Gaelg."*

I had read Reverend Kelly's 1780 <u>Manx Grammar</u>. I had read some Manx material Adrian recommended to me, and even listened to a few bits of spoken Manx. Unfortunately, such studies did not immediately prepare me for actual conversation. I heard my name. I heard the name of my city. I heard *Gaelg,* which is Manx's name for its own language. The rest of the introduction went over my head.

The younger woman spoke easily. Her speech was rather fluent, only occasionally halting as she searched for words. The older woman (who I learned was the younger woman's mother) spoke with some difficulty, frequently injecting English words into fragments of Manx sentences.

The older man, his eyes fixed intently on his half-empty pint, did not seem to understand Manx at all. Adrian would pose a question in Manx (speaking especially slowly, it seemed). The question would be met with an empty stare. When Adrian explained his questions in English, the man's responses seemed to be English injected conservatively with Manx. Adrian would shake his head and continue with the lesson.

Adrian turned to address the two women. The man took a long sip and turned to me.

"Don't understand a word, you know." The man was practically bald, and had a distinct dreariness about him. "I'm Kevin. What'd he say your name was?" Kevin nodded his head toward Adrian.

"I'm Nick."

"Nick, izzit? And what brings you all the way here?"

"I'm studying Manx, actually. I'm mostly researching its endangerment and its restoration—"

"Are you now? The endangerment. Well, then..." Kevin finished his pint off in a single sip, took a deep breath and turned toward me. "My name is Kevin Woodworth. Do you know the name? Woodworth?"

"I don't think I do, actually."

"Well." Kevin stood up clumsily, nearly knocking over his empty glass. "I've got something I have to get for you. I'll have to walk to my house. It's right up the street, so I'll be back—" Kevin struggled to put his arm through the sleeve of his jacket—"just a few minutes."

"Are you sure it isn't too much trouble? Shouldn't you stay for the lesson?"

Kevin scoffed. "I don't understand a word anyway."

Adrian turned to address a question to Kevin. "Getting another pint, Kevin?" Adrian asked with a smile.

"No," Kevin replied defiantly. "I'm going home." His speech was slurred and slow. "Walking home, for what it's worth."

"He's coming right back," I explained. "He said he wanted to get something for me after I said I was researching Manx."

"Is my lesson not holding your interest, Kevin?"

"How am I s'posed to take interest if I can't understand a fucking word—"

"Okay, off you go Kevin." Adrian took a quick sip from his coke and turned back to the two women. Kevin stumbled his way to the door of the pub and disappeared into the rainy night.

I listened carefully to the lesson. "*Ta me gobbraghey anys Doolish. Anys yn...* shop? How do you say 'shop' again?" the older woman said. I remembered that *Doolish* is the Manx name for Douglas and that *ta me* conjugates the verb of the sentence in the first person. I picked up that *Anys* means "in," *yn* means "the," and, since the woman must have been a shopkeeper, *gobbraghey* must mean "to work."

As the conversations went on, the words became demystified. Either from Manx words that I had already learned or from English words that the women injected into their speech, I was able to deduce more and more vocabulary. By the end of the lesson, their sentences began to unravel for me. It was the wonderful feeling I got one day in 8th grade Spanish class when I no longer had to translate my teacher's words in my head. Or when I was in the middle of *Survive Style 5+*, a Japanese film I was watching to practice the language, and I realized that the subtitles were telling me what I already knew. Like riding a bicycle without training wheels for the first time, I could try to follow the dialog with my ears alone. It's what Steven Pinker calls the "comprehension point," and, with Manx, it started in Mad Dog's pub.

Although I was still far from understanding complex sentences at this point (let alone from creating my own sentences or holding passable conversation), it was a sliver of hope. I had confidence, then, that I would be able to learn Manx.

Adrian cleared his throat. "*Feer vie, feer vie.* That'll do it for today, I'd say—Where did Kevin get to? Well, good enough." Adrian turned toward me. "Hope you enjoyed yourself, Nick."

"Yeah! I picked up on quite a lot."

"Good good. So what're you studying exactly, then?" I explained my main objectives and mentioned my interview with Brian earlier in the day. Adrian perked up. "You're not just another reporter come trying to save some poor country folks then."

"Sorry?"

"These folks come through here every once in a blue moon. Heard that Manx has fifty some-odd speakers left and they imagine hoards of Manx people dying or something. So you want to know about the revival as well, then?"

"Yes, definitely."

"I'll be teaching a Manx lesson to some young folks tomorrow afternoon at Castle Rushen elementary school. You'd be interested to see it, I think." A clank sounded from the door as Kevin stumbled in, his hair dripping onto the hardwood floor.

"*I'm back!*" he shouted across the pub. The bartender gave him a sidelong glance, and looked knowingly toward Adrian.

"Well, I should be off then." Adrian stood and put his coat on. "You've missed the lesson again, Kevin." Kevin paid no attention to the comment and reclaimed his seat. He reached into his jacket pocket and pulled a folded newspaper clipping from his jacket pocket. I unfolded it on the table. The article was water stained and the pictures were dripping ink.

"Norwegian professor records Joseph Woodworth, the last living voice of Man," the headline read.

Castle Rushen.

EIGHT

Joseph Woodworth was born in 1853 in Port Erin (*Purt Charin* in Manx). His parents spoke no English at all but, when he started working in the town's docks at twelve, he picked up English from the British and Irish merchants who frequented the port. He married a woman named Margaret in 1882, and the couple had a healthy baby girl, Violet Woodworth, in 1888. Like most Manx parents of the time, Margaret and Joseph decided to raise their daughter in an entirely English household to assure that the child would not have to suffer the lowered social status that came attached to an association with Manx, thus securing respect and success for Violet in her adulthood.

When Professor Carl J.S. Marstrander, the professor of Celtic Studies at Oslo University, visited the Island in the summer of 1929, Joseph had not spoken Manx in over 40 years. Few people spoke Manx in the late 1920s (and those who did wouldn't dare admit it, as doing so would reveal that the speaker's parents were poor or unsophisticated). This social stigma became a challenge to Marstrander as he attempted to track down the last living Manx speakers. Of the Island's 60,000 inhabitants, Marstrander found five Manx speakers: 79-year-old Thomas Christian of Ramsey, 80-year-old Bernard Crebbin of Bradda, 81-year-old Harry Kelly of Cregneash, 83-year-old William Quane of Peel, and 76-year-old Joseph Woodworth of Port Erin.

Marstrander recognized that older Manx speakers were not passing their language on to younger generations. Since the youngest of Manx's remaining speakers was 76 (well past the upper limits of life expectancy in 1929), Professor Marstrander wasted no time documenting the language: he recorded Manx speech and conversations on almost one hundred wax cylinders.

Joseph Woodworth had no taste for modern technology. He took the professor fishing in the local docks. He told him that, when he was a boy, Chicken Rock was called *Carrick Vooar* (literally "big rock"). That a rock shaped like a nose, called *Y Troin Wuigh* ("yellow nose") between Port Erin and Niarbyl used to be his fishing mark. That the narrow cove near Bradda Hill was called *Lag ny Sker* ("hollow of the Sker").

Marstrander took his wax recordings home to Oslo. Unfortunately, the professor's attic did little to shield the wax recordings from the harsh

Norweigen winters (or the Second World War), and many of the recordings perished. The recordings that survived have been transferred to compact disc and, along with Brian Stowell's recordings, comprise the remaining recordings of original Manx speech.

In 1931, two years after Marstrander's visit, Joseph Woodworth passed away in his home in Port Erin. By 1936, none of Marstrander's Manx speakers was alive. In fact, no one knew of any living Manx speaker. (Ned Maddrell, Brian Stowell's mentor, apparently learned Manx from his father, but Maddrell Sr. and Maddrell Jr.'s proficiencies in the language were unknown to the world at the time).

As far as anyone could tell, Manx had been replaced completely by English on the Isle of Man. The Island saw no genocide, disease or exodus (in fact, the population enjoyed a steady increase while Manx's speakership suffered a rapid decrease). The Manx people simply *wanted* to speak English. English meant business with British merchants while Manx meant admitting one's poverty. English meant education and career opportunities in Douglas—"the city"—while Manx meant a life secluded among the agricultural folk in the countryside. Learning English was simply good for business.

NINE

I woke the next morning to the clock bell (the fourth ring of six, for what it's worth). The mist was coating the cricket greens, and the outside world looked cold, heavy, and unfriendly.

I had met the Liverpool University students briefly after returning from Mad Dog's pub the night before. They introduced themselves one by one, but in my exhaustion, I doubted my ability to remember their names upon a second meeting. I decided that breakfast would be something of a test. Or, at least a test of my ability to address others without using their names. After a too-cold shower, I threw on some clothes and made my way into the kitchen.

The kitchen was bustling. Silverware clanked loudly against china from one end, and a group of students stood anxiously around a teapot on the stove at the other. As I entered, a small hush filled the room. A few students looked over their shoulders, shooting brief glances at me. A short silence ensued.

A boy with short, brown hair smiled and yelled at me, "Hey, it's Nick, right? Come sit, mate." Chris was one name I was able to put a face with: he took great pains to introduce himself, which was a courtesy I appreciated. "How'd ya sleep? Hard to get a wink with the bells and all. And I heard the Duke of Lancaster's regiment is bussing in tonight—"

"That's just a rumor, Chris." A short boy with a ponytail slinked into a chair. He extended his arm, presenting me with his hand the way I would have expected the Queen of England to present herself. "I'm Tim." I shook his hand, which he quickly retracted, craning his neck toward the window instead.

"So what's on your agenda for today, mate?" Chris asked.

"Well, I'm going to this elementary school nearby to sit in on a Manx class. See how they feel about learning Manx, things like that"

"Probably they vill not like it," a boy in the corner interjected. He was tall and thin, and had long, blonde hair covering his long, pale face. He stared intently into his tea as he stirred it with a spoon and spoke with an accent I couldn't place. "When I vas growing up, I was made to learn Russian and I did not take to it."

"Where did you grow up?" I asked.

"Estonia." He looked up. "Vere else? Estonia of course."

A girl with short blonde hair and glasses spoke up. "This is Rain." She looked at me apologetically, then extended her hand. "I'm Ellie. We all think it's quite interesting what you're doing. We all know about this island, of course, but I never knew they had their own language."

Chris nodded in agreement.

"Yes, it is a Goidelic language," Rain replied. He was still fixed on his teacup. "This is correct, no?"

"Yeah, that's right... You know about Manx, huh?"

"I know that it is a Goidelic language, it seems." His spoon made a soft clinking against his cup. A slight pause ensued.

Tim broke the silence. "Well, I'm going outside for a smoke. I don't suppose anyone will join me?" The students shook their heads, and Tim slunk off.

I turned toward Chris. "So, what are you guys doing, exactly?"

"Well, we walk toward Rushen Abbey and excavate this small bit of it that they've only just discovered."

"Rushen Abbey... That must be near Rushen Castle, right?"

"It's about a twenty-minute walk," Ellie replied. "One of the Viking rulers had them both built. Castle Rushen was where the king lived until Robert the Bruce took it over, actually."

"Singlehandedly," piped Rain. The students were beginning to shuffle out.

"Well, we have to get off to work or we'll be late," said Chris. Rain gulped down what was left of his tea, and the flock of students walked off into the fog outside.

Left inside the room was a middle-aged man and an old woman, both of whom had apparently become Max's audience.

"When I was younger I'd ride them myself, but those days are gone, they are. Ah, hello there Chris!"

"Oh, I'm Nick actually—"

"Chris, this is Steven, and this is Eva."

"Nice to meet you, Nick," the man said with a wink. Max got up to clean up the disaster zone that the Liverpool students left in the kitchen. "I hear you're here to study Manx." I was surprised to discover that Steven spoke with an Australian accent.

"That's right. You know of it?" I asked.

"Sure I do. I was raised here, you know. Right here, in Castletown. I studied here at King Bill's when I was young. Colbourne House. My parents moved us to Melbourne when I was sixteen and I've lived there since. But sure, I know about Manx. It was the thing my parents never talked about," he said with a laugh.

"Manx? Never 'erd of it meself," Eva said. Her voice was deep and gruff, presumably from years of smoking. "What do you study, Nick?" she asked.

"Well, I'm not in college yet, but I'm planning on studying linguistics."

"Linguistics izzit. If I 'ad to do it over I'd become a doctor. If I knew what a racket those doctors made, I'dve studied medicine. No doubt of it." A brief silence ensued as the three of us stared out at the world through the window. A band of green supporting a mass of dense white above it: the view through the window looked like a modern art piece. As we pondered the scene, a distant train whistle cut swiftly through the silence.

I was due at the Elementary School in just under an hour, so I politely excused myself and walked out of the kitchen and into the foggy island outside.

TEN

After a few helpful index-finger points from locals, I found my way past the muddy harbor that Castle Rushen overlooks, through a narrow alleyway, and into a large, fenced-in area with the words "Castle Rushen Elementary School" engraved in stone outside it.

Toe-headed boys and girls dressed in navy sport jackets and white button-down shirts (both genders identical in uniform except that the boys wore red ties while the girls sported navy bows) pranced around a playground, kicking a soccer ball or lounging about on the grass.

Inside the main building, Adrian sat on a bench, twiddling his thumbs nervously. He noticed me, and his hand shot up above the heads of the children who filed through the halls.

"Hey there, Nick," he said with a smile.

"Sorry I'm late. I got a bit lost…"

"Quite alright. Are you all ready to go, then?"

"All ready."

He nodded. "Good enough." Adrian led me through a maze of hallways into an ordinary classroom: spelling and arithmetic posters plastered against the wall, and the children's drawings hung from the ceiling on strings. The teacher, an elderly woman, introduced herself as Mrs. Dawkins.

Adrian began drawing props from his duffel bag and setting them on a table: a ball, some large, colorful numbers and a few stuffed animals populated the desktop. I produced my tape recorder from my jacket pocket and asked Mrs. Dawkins if I could ask a few questions before the children came in.

"Oh, certainly, what would you like to know?" Ms Dawkins said with a smile.

"So, what age are these kids, exactly?"

"Oh, these are 5th years, so they're all about 10 and 11, about."

"So they learn Manx early."

She laughed. "Well, I suppose… This is part of a larger Manx education course. It covers government, some ancient history, modern history, all of that. This is actually the first year Manx language is part of the curriculum, actually."

"Wait, so you've been teaching a course on Manx history without teaching the language?"

Mrs. Dawkins nodded knowingly. "Yes, we actually never mentioned the Manx language before."

"How long has the school been teaching this course?"

"Oh, it's not just Castle Rushen. It's required all throughout the Isle. It's been taught for…" She turned toward Adrian, addressing the question to him. "Ten years? Twelve?"

"Must be around there, I'd say," Adrian responded as he ordered the cartoonish numbers on the table.

"Well, we're not quite sure how the children will respond to Manx, really. I suppose you're seeing history in the making, then." She smiled and adjusted her glasses. Within minutes, children began to storm into the classroom, laughing and running. Mrs. Dawkins stood up and cast a gentle, quiet presence upon the children. With the sort of magic that can only come from years of experience, the children's expressions changed instantly to a mellow, transfixed calm.

"Today, we have a special visitor. This is Adrian Cain." Adrian smiled and waved energetically. "Adrian is going to teach us about the Manx language. How many of you have heard of Manx?" The children sat like statues. One child scratched his nose. Another began to stare up toward the ceiling. Adrian scratched his head nervously and began to speak.

"Well, long ago, everyone on the Island spoke Manx. Most of your great, great grandparents probably spoke no English at all."

A girl interjected, "My family's all from London."

Mrs. Dawkins threw a stern look, holding her finger to her lips.

"Anyway, very few people speak Manx now-a-days," Adrian continued. "So, today we'll learn a bit of Manx. How does that sound?" The children's faces expressed idle curiosity. Adrian paused and, after he realized that his audience was not going to respond, he began his lesson.

Mrs. Dawkins allowed me to record video from the corner of the classroom. The children appeared to pay no attention to me at all as Adrian began his lesson: he started by saying a few basic greetings and expressions and prompting the children to repeat after him: m*oghrey mie* (good morning), *fastyr mie* (good afternoon), *bannaghtyn* (blessings) and so on. Adrian went through the large, plastic numbers and named the toy animals in Manx, all of which the children seemed to enjoy. The magic came, however, when Adrian increased the lesson's complexity.

Adrian started by teaching a few simple words: the words for "door," "table," and "seat," and the verbs "to go," "to sit," "to stand" and "to turn oneself around," and the adverbs "slowly" and "quickly." The children had just learned a few simple words, and I doubted that a group of ten- and eleven-year-olds would be able to properly comprehend instructions in a foreign language.

Adrian picked a girl out of the class (ironically, the same girl who stated that her parents were from London). "*Irree*," Adrian said. The girl stood up. "*Goll ec yn dorrys.*" The girl began to walk to the door. "*Dy tappee!*" Adrian yelled after her. The girl quickened her pace. "*Braew, braew. Soie sheese.*" The girl sat on the floor directly in front of the door, much to the amusement of her classmates. Adrian smiled and rolled his eyes. *"Soie sheese ec yn boayrd."* The girl picked herself up, walked back to her desk, and sat proudly in her seat.

The lesson was repeated with four more students, each of whom easily understood and complied with Adrian's Manx instructions. Contrary to my expectations, a group of ten- and eleven-year-olds *was* able to understand instruction in Manx, and appeared to do so with little effort at all.

At my request, Mrs. Dawkins pulled aside a few children for me to interview. Two girls (one of whom was Adrian's first victim) and one boy stayed behind as their classmates shuffled out of the room.

"Well, thank you all for sitting down with me," I said. The children all nodded happily. "So, could you all tell me your names and ages?"

"I'm Sarah and I'm eleven," said the first girl.

"I'm Will and I'm twelve," said the boy.

"I'm Jessica and I'm eleven," said the last girl with a distinctly British accent.

"So, is this your first time learning Manx?" I asked the children.

They all nodded.

"Well, I knew bits from my grandparents," Will said.

"Really? Did your grandparents speak Manx?"

"I don't think so. They just knew the basic things. Like 'good morning' and all that. That's what they told me anyway."

Adrian teaching at Castle Rushen Elemntary School.

"Why do you think you learn about Manx in school?" I asked. The children sat and thought for a moment.

"Probably to learn the culture of our Island," said Sarah.

"Yes, to see where we come from," Will added.

"Where you come from? How so?"

"You know, to see what we were like before everything."

"Everything?"

"Yeah. The British and all." Jessica appeared to pay the comment no mind, and I moved on.

"Do you think you'd be interested in learning Manx when you're older? As a teenager, or even as an adult?"

Sarah shrugged her shoulders. "Maybe."

"Yes, that would be fun. I'd like to speak Manx," Will answered.

It was Jessica's enthusiastic response, however, that surprised me the most. "Yes, I'd like to learn Manx, too."

"Even though your parents are British?" I asked.

"Well, yes, but... I'm being raised here. So I'm as Manx as anyone, aren't I?" I couldn't help but break into a smile.

I thanked Sarah, Will and Jessica for their time. The three children ran out of the room and bounced happily toward their next classes. Mrs.

Dawkins asked me how the interview went, and I said that her children were quite wonderful and thanked her profusely for the opportunity.

Outside the school's gates, Adrian was just hanging up his phone. "How did your interview go?" he asked.

"Very well! You'll be pleased to learn that they all said they'd like to learn Manx later, actually. Even that girl who said her parents were from London."

Adrian smiled broadly. "Well, glad to hear all that. Find out anything else interesting?"

"A few things here and there, yes. Really, what surprised me was how quickly the kids picked up the Manx. I mean, they were understanding sentences, weren't they?"

Adrian laughed. "Magic of youth, innit?" He gave a glance back toward the school. "Like little sponges, you know? They'll retain anything." He looked back. "Tell me, have you heard of Bunscoill Ghaelgagh?"

"The all-Manx school? I have, yes."

"Why don't you stop by there Wednesday. If you really want to see kids doing some magic. All speak proper natural Manx there, yessir." Adrian asked if I needed a ride back to King William's. I told him I'd walk, and we bid our farewells.

I stood outside the school's gate. Castle Rushen rose above the modest buildings in the distance. Children played behind me, screaming and laughing on the playground equipment. One day, perhaps, their seventeen-year-old selves will be standing outside the gates of their former elementary school, listening to the next generation of children screaming. Perhaps they'll speak Manx.

The screams continued, but the world was quiet where I stood.

ELEVEN

I got back to King William's at noon. A light blue had broken through the gray, and I decided that a few hours of peace and quiet would do me good.

I hadn't been in bed for more than five minutes before I heard a van pull to a stop outside. Boots thumped against concrete. Men grunted and barked. I shot up and ran to the door.

As soon as I arrived at the doorway, the door burst open. Men—a platoon of monstrous, broad-shouldered beasts—swarmed into the dormitory in a cloud of camouflage green. A short, stocky man barked orders from behind them. Within thirty seconds, the soldiers had disappeared up the stairs with their duffel bags. The man walked over to me.

"Do you know where Max is?" he asked.

"Oh, I think he's upstairs. Just take the stairs, go left—"

"What are you? Canadian?"

"Oh. I'm American. Anyway—" The man turned his head away from me sharply and disappeared up the stairs.

I retreated to my room and collapsed onto my bed. My exhaustion forced my eyes shut almost immediately. The slam of my room's door opened them a few minutes later. Chris stood in the threshold.

"So the army's boarding up here, are they?" he said. I rolled over and directed my voice in his general direction.

"Looks like it."

"Well, I'm not staying here with those army blokes." He paused. "Ellie and I want to go exploring. Want to come?"

"Exploring? Exploring where?"

"I don't know, the Island. It's not a big place. We'll be able to see most of it by sundown." He smiled.

"I should really stay in bed," I began.

"Well, I see *you* have no sense of adventure," Chris responded. Half an hour later, Ellie, Chris and I were crammed into the cabin of a steam train bound for Port Erin.

As soon as we stepped off our train, we were thrashed by a harsh wind that threatened to knock us off our feet. I took a look around.

Port Erin is a stretch of seashore lined with buildings cascading crowdedly across a cliff like a group of children leaning over a game of marbles. The whites and light-blues of the buildings seemed to drift upward toward the mariner's sky, and the sounds of waves beating against craggy rocks flowed to our ears. A fierce wind whipped across the sea, whistling through the streets and alleys of the village.

"Thanks for getting me out of bed, Chris," I said.

"Anytime, mate." We spent a few silent moments surveying our surroundings, deciding what to do. Chris looked toward the shore, dotted with beached jellyfish waiting patiently for the high tide. My eyes wandered down a narrow street lined with shops. Signs protruded from the storefronts: "Public House," "Antiques," "Sporting Goods," "Clocks: Built and Repaired."

I felt a tap on my shoulder from Ellie. Her pointer finger followed her gaze along the coastline. "What do you imagine that is?"

My eyes traced along a winding dirt path that was draped across the shoreline like a string. The path twisted and turned in and out of sight, leading to a tower perched upon a mountain peak. The peak on which the tower rested slid into the cliff. Waves beat against its sharp rock face and birds soared above the crenellated turret.

"Looks like quite a walk," Chris said.

The image of the tower, graceful and mysterious against a rushing, windy sky, erased my fatigue and restored my sense of adventure. "I'm up for a walk. How about you guys?" I said.

Walking is always fun when I get started. The first ten minutes of a long walk make me wonder why I don't walk more often. Why I don't incorporate walking into my everyday routine. The next twenty minutes make me wonder why I don't exercise more as my feet start to protest under their strain. The remaining time makes me increasingly foul-tempered as I struggle against my body's complaints. We decided to rest at a cliff about a hundred feet from our destination.

We sat with our feet dangling off the cliff. The soles of our shoes looked a few hundred feet down into the turbulent water, and our eyes drifted out into the distance with the tide.

"We can probably see Ireland if we look hard enough," Ellie said. We leaned in and squinted but couldn't find Ireland in the horizon. We sat in silence for a few moments before continuing our climb.

Heather grew at the foot of the tower, and a small sign stood before the entrance: "The owners are not responsible for injury."

"One way to go from here, innit," Chris said. It was pitch dark inside the tower's spiral staircase. There wasn't a single window. We trekked up, following the sound of our own footsteps until a shaft of light appeared, slanting through an opening above us.

Chris finds his footing on the hills of Port Erin.

We emerged above the village, floating above the island itself. The wind pierced through us but the spire held us steady, closer to heaven. On one side, cliffs and buildings leaned into the beach, sliding cautiously down the steep hills. On the other side, the sea extended like a blanket outward into infinity.

Chris let out a scream. Ellie let out a scream. I let out a scream. Our yells burst outward and reverberated over the hill, over the village, perhaps over the whole Island, perhaps to the coast of Ireland we could not see. The wind carried it as if by magic and our sounds flew around us and through us and beyond us, and, when we finally descended the spiral staircase, we knew that we were not the same people who climbed it.

The tower approaches in the distance in Port Erin.

TWELVE

The tower that looks over Port Erin is called Milner's Tower. It was constructed upon the summit of Bradda Head in 1871 to commemorate William Milner, owner of a famous safe-making company. His safes were made from Manx metal, mined on the Island itself, which Milner thought to be the finest metal on the planet.

In the first half of the 19th century, a Manx person could pick from two industries: agriculture or shipping. Neither was particularly profitable, and the Island's population grew faster than its opportunities did. The beginning of the mining industry supported by William Milner was the Island's first major step toward a thriving economy.

Mining and metal-based products remained the Island's largest industry until 1866 when Tynwald negotiated a degree of Home Rule with the British Crown. For the first time since the Vikings landed on the Isle of Man early in the first millennium, the Manx government was able to set its own taxes and tariffs. From 1866 to the 1950s, the Isle of Man became a premier holiday destination for the British. English customers flocked to the Isle's shores in huge numbers by ferry, conquering the beaches as native Manx catered to their luxurious vacations. Liverpudlian singer George Formby captured the British enthusiasm for Manx tourism during the turn of the 20th century:

> *There's a beautiful spot called the Isle of Man*
> *Where holiday folk like to go.*
> *But just how it came*
> *To be given that name,*
> *Really I'd like to know.*
> *Crowds of spinsters over forty*
> *Simply dying to be naughty*
> *And they call it the Isle of Man.*

Previously, Brits were confined to major ports and docks. They unloaded their cargo, paraded around the shipping villages and returned to sea, rarely venturing inland. Most people in or around shipping ports (a significant portion of the Island's population) needed to know English to successfully interact with British merchants and sailors (and therefore receive valuable British currency), but other Manx people had no real need for English, most likely contributing to the increased use of Manx among agricultural communities.

After tourism took hold, however, British tourists began leaving the confines of port cities. Residents of scenic inland villages had to communicate with the English speaking visitors. Traditional craft-workers went into the business of making handmade souvenirs with English words on them. In this era, good English meant good business, and Manx was in no one's best interest. This new, more widespread need for English on the Island is most likely responsible for the extreme drop in Manx speakers in the early 20th century, and accounts for why Joseph Woodward was one of the few people who still spoke Manx in the era of surging tourism on the Island.

After the 1950s, airplane travel became more economically feasible and many English and Irish tourists opted for continental European vacation spots with sunnier climates than the Isle of Man (particularly Spain and Greece). The tourism industry took a turn for the worse, and by the 1970s, hardly anyone visited the Island on holiday. The collapse of tourism devastated the Manx economy and, with no British government to support the Island in hard economic times, the Island had to negotiate rocky financial waters.

In the 1970s, Tynwald responded to the crisis by removing taxes completely and instating a "don't ask, don't tell" policy regarding banking and money transfer. Locals refer jokingly to the policy as "no tax, no tariffs, no questions." This policy attracted a great number of powerful, global banks: institutions such as HSBC and Zurich Bank International Ltd.

relocated their offshore banking headquarters from distant Caribbean islands to the more conveniently located Isle of Man. The residents of the Island (all of whom were English-speaking at this point) made productive (and inexpensive) employees, and attracted a tremendous amount of immigration from the United Kingdom. Today, only about a third of the Island's population is ethnically Manx; the other two-thirds (about 53,000 of the Island's 80,000 residents) are non-Manx (mostly British, Scottish and Irish). An already decaying sense of Manx heritage was further weakened by an influx of non-Manx (and, in the case of the English, non-Celtic) ethnicities, and little interest in Manx language or culture remained on the Island.

By anyone's estimation, Manx's death seemed permanent. All native speakers were deceased and, to make Manx's future more grim, few people seemed to care. In 1999, however, a group of parents approached the Island's Department of Education and requested that the government fund a Manx-language elementary school. Convincing a government with a thirty-year history of extremely conservative fiscal policy to fund a school that teaches a dead language is not an easy task. After three years, Bunscoill Ghaelgagh (literally, Manx School) opened in a few rooms of the Ballacotier School in Douglas. Two years later, its enrollment grew so much that it was forced to relocate to a new building across from Tynwald Hill in St. John's.

Bunscoill currently enrolls forty-six children ages five to twelve. The children learn every subject entirely in Manx, and are usually fluent by the end of their first year (at age six or seven). These forty-six children

Banks mix with classic buildings in Douglas.

comprise almost 80% of the language's fifty-four speakers. What is more
amazing, however, is that only four or five people (including Brian Stowell
and Adrian Cain) spoke Manx before Bunscoill opened its doors. Today,
not only are a significant number of children learning Manx, but a
significant number of parents are expressing interest in raising bilingual
children. Throughout most of the 20th century, Manx was not on anyone's
mind: during the first half of the 20th century, Manx people preferred to
pretend that Manx never existed and, during the latter half of the century,
no one seemed to remember or care about the lost language. The 21st
century, however, has seen the Manx people renew their interest in the
Manx language, and a tongue has truly been resurrected from the dead.

This complete change in public opinion came suddenly and
without warning. What caused an entire Island to change its mind about
the importance of its language? What can account for this massive surge in
interest? For the answer, I went to the Bunscoill itself.

Thirteen

I stood near the front of the red double-decker bus, clutching a bright yellow handrail as the bus bounced along the road. The brakes squeaked as the bus squealed to a stop, and the doors slid open.

"Tynwald Hill," the driver yelled back. I thanked him and hopped off the bus. Outside, the cold hung in the air. It clung to my fingers, and the street was still wet from Tuesday night's rain. I stood facing a grass mound sculpted from the earth itself: it consisted of a few circular platforms stacked on top of one another, each smaller than the one below it. Tynwald Parliament had its meetings on this oddly shaped amphitheater for much of its 1000-year history, only moving to the Legislative Building in Douglas relatively recently. Across from Tynwald Hill stood a modest, wooden

Bunscoill Ghaelgagh.

building with a sign in front: "Bunscoill Ghaelgagh." I crossed the quiet street and stepped through the threshold. Almost immediately, a smiling, middle-aged woman emerged into the hallway and greeted me.

"Oh hello! You must be Nick, yes?"

"Yes, I am—"

"Oh good, Adrian told me you were coming today. I'm Julie Matthews, and I run the school here. So you'd like to see the school at work, I suppose?" She gave a little laugh.

"Well, yes, that would be great."

"Good, good. Here, follow me." The woman led me through the hallway into a small breakfast nook in the back of the building. She gestured toward a couch, decorated with a faded, floral pattern. I sat, and she put a teakettle on the stove. "Is black tea alright?"

"Well—"

"I'll warn you before you answer that it's all we have." She laughed and sat down in a chair across from me. "So, what would you like to know?"

"Well, let's see…" I flipped frantically through my notebook, trying to find the questions I had written for Julie. "So, every subject is taught entirely in Manx here?"

"That's right. Except for English, of course," Julie said with a smile.

"What made you want to learn Manx? And what brought you to teaching it?"

"Well, I learned it with Adrian and Brain like everyone else. But it was really seeing the parents unite back in 1998 and 1999—back when there was the fight to get this school started—that's when I really became interested in *teaching* Manx, you know. Just seeing everyone all excited about it, I suppose."

"So, how would you gauge the general population's enthusiasm for Manx, then?"

"Well, enthusiasm or awareness? I've seen public awareness grow exponentially, really—you know, even twenty years ago, it would be difficult to find someone who knew about Manx at all. And today mostly everyone has at least a vague understanding of a Manx language that existed here before English came. As far as enthusiasm goes... Well, I don't see a line of people coming to learn Manx. But there are certainly enough parents who want their children to learn. And we have kids here with only one Manx parent, or even two foreign-born parents in a few cases. So it varies, I'd say." An older woman with short, gray hair entered the room.

"Hello! Are you the researcher? I'm Kate Pitts," the woman said with a rich Scottish accent. Despite the odd sensation that came with hearing myself referred to as a "researcher," I stood to greet Kate and introduced myself. "Well, I teach the first-years here. So I take it you'd like to sit in on our class?"

Kate led me into a typical-looking kindergarten classroom down the hall. Finger paintings were plastered onto the wall, and pictures of animals dangled from the ceiling. Children dressed in bright blue sweaters sat around tables and read from picture books. Underneath the finger paintings, however, were Manx words. The animals that hung from the ceiling had masking tape over their English names with their Manx names written in marker on top. English picture books were pasted over with Manx words. A young girl approached Kate and tugged at her shirt.

"*Bnr Pitts? Craad ta* bag?"

"*Ta'n sac ec yn tayrnag, Christie,*" Kate replied. The girl ran over to a drawer, opened it and grabbed her bag from inside. Kate turned to me. "You see? The children replace Manx words they don't know with English words. So we just use the proper Manx and they pick it up after a while. Just yesterday, a boy didn't know the word for 'book,' but he had to say 'books' in a sentence so he said '*bookyn.*' Declined it as if it were a Manx word. The kids are really quite clever."

Kate offered me a seat in the middle of the room. On one side of the room, three younger children constructed houses from building blocks. They did so in complete silence, apparently able to coordinate their movements without language at all. On the other side of the room, a boy and girl tugged on a ball of string. Kate walked over and muttered something I couldn't make out to the children. Suddenly, the boy and the girl began to negotiate in Manx. The boy would made an offer. The girl rejected the offer and proposed a counter-offer. The boy added a term to the counter-offer. The girl accepted, and the boy took the ball of yarn and ran off. Kate looked at the children and smiled.

"They get on quite well, don't they?" she said.

"So, I can't help but notice that you have a Scottish accent... How did you learn Manx, exactly?"

"Keen ear for an American! You are American, right? Not Canadian? I can never tell the difference."

"No no, I'm American," I laughed.

"Well, I moved here from Glasgow, and I had been involved with the Scottish Gaelic movement there a bit. I suppose I couldn't help but get into it, and when I heard that there was a whole group of people who wanted to make this school happen… Well, it inspired me to really learn Manx, I suppose."

"Do you mind if I talk to some of your students?" I asked.

"Not at all. Here in fact, you can talk to Christie." Kate called Christie over to me.

"Hello, Christie. I'm Nick, and I'm here from the United States studying Manx," I told her.

"Hello! Would you like to see my picture?"

"Sure, why not?" Christie showed me a picture of a pig with the word *muick* underneath it. I complimented her artistry and continued with my questions. "So, how old are you?"

"Five!" she replied.

"And this is your first year here?"

"Of course! I'm a first year."

"Do your parents speak any Manx?"

"Nope!" Christie replied.

"And how about your grandparents?"

Kate's class at work in Bunscoill.

"No, not at all! They actually aren't as keen on me learning... My parents wanted to send me here but my grandparents said I oughtn't learn Manx and that it would confuse me, but my parents were quite insistent."

"Well, if a movie came out in Manx," I asked, "do you think many people would go see it?"

"Yes, of course they would! Lots of people. Everyone here at the school. Maybe outside the Island too." At that moment, a girl ran over to Christie and whispered something in her ear. Christie giggled and turned toward me. "I've got to go, sorry!" Christie ran off after the other girl.

After a few minutes, Julie escorted me into the older children's room. She explained that these children were ten to twelve, and would be graduating the following year to go on to middle school.

A group of children were huddled around a young, bearded man. The man, no older than twenty-five, held a white board and spoke excitedly to the children in Manx as he spelled words in erasable marker.

"Paul, this is Nick. Nick, Paul Rogers."

"Nice to meet you, Nick. I was just teaching some spelling. Manx spelling is quite tricky, you know."

"I've noticed, actually..." Manx words often look like gibberish on first glance, as they are usually stacked with uncommon (in English at least) combinations of consonants and vowels. "So, how long have you been teaching here?"

"Oh, since the school started. I moved here from Wales before the whole revival happened, really."

"From Wales?"

"Yes—believe it or not, I learnt Welsh before Manx."

"Really? What got you interested in Manx?"

"Well, I married a Manx woman, of course," Paul smiled.

"Does your wife speak Manx?"

"Not really, no. But I learned about the Island through her, and I got interested in the culture. So here I am." Maps plastered the wall behind Paul. Next to his desk, two guitars (one acoustic and one electric) were propped up on guitar stands. "Well, would you like to sit down and speak with a few of the kids?" Paul asked.

Paul set me up in a corner of the room. He gave me a swiveling office chair and placed a smaller, kid-sized chair across from me.

My first interviewee was a blonde-haired girl who introduced herself as Jenny. I took out my tape recorder, introduced myself and began recording.

"Have you been studying here at Bunscoill since you were young?" I asked. Jennifer gave a glance to Paul.

"You can speak in English," Paul assured her.

"Yes, since the earliest year," she answered.

"Do your parents speak any Manx?"

"No, they don't know a word."

"How about your grandparents?"

Jennifer thought for a moment. "I think they know a few words, but I'm the first to speak Manx I think."

"So why do you think your parents wanted you to go to Bunscoill?"

Jennifer cocked her head and looked at me ponderously. "I don't know really…"

"Do you think your parents would have wanted to learn Manx at your age?"

"Well, they're quite keen on it now," Jennifer said.

"Do you have any idea why they didn't learn Manx when they were your age?"

Jennifer took another long pause to think. I was surprised at her willingness to answer difficult questions. "Well, I don't think it was done then. To learn Manx, I mean." Jennifer was obviously more aware than an average ten-year-old.

"Do you know why?" I asked.

"Not really. It just seems like the older folks never learned Manx. I suppose we're the first where it's alright," she said.

"If a movie came out in Manx, do you think a lot of people would see it?"

"No, I don't. Hardly anyone seems to speak Manx. Except our teachers of course."

"Do you think more people will speak when you're older?"

Jennifer looked upward, as if adding numbers in her head. "Maybe. But still not as much as English."

I couldn't help but smile at Jennifer's keen perception. I thanked her for her time.

The next child to take the seat across from me was a boy with thin-rimmed glasses and a blue beanie.

"What's your name?" I asked.

"Peter."

"And have you been at Bunscoill for all of primary school, Peter?"

Peter nodded.

"So, Peter. When you're with your friends from school, do you speak with them in Manx or English."

"Oh, usually English. Unless we don't want adults to understand us, then we speak in Manx. They look at us like we're crazy though."

"Have you ever spoken to anyone in Manx who wasn't from Bunscoill?" Peter shook his head. Having run out of questions, I thanked Peter for his time. Before Paul fetched the next child, I had something to investigate.

Contrary to what many English teachers may say, slang is a vital part of human language. The creation of slang indicates a thriving, living language: a tongue that does not change, after all, is a tongue that will not survive. In fact, the prevalence of slang is a simple way of assessing the vitality of a language as it often indicates a regular, vernacular use. In between interviews, I decided to bring the matter up with Paul.

"Do you ever hear the kids using slang words? Or perhaps versions of words you're not familiar with?"

"Well, besides mixing in English words where they don't belong..." Paul smiled, "No, all of our students have clean mouths. I don't think they'd invent any words themselves, really."

My own early childhood is in recent memory and, if my ten-year-old self learned a slang word, I certainly wouldn't share it with my teacher.

A blonde-haired, gray-eyed girl sat down in front of me. Again, I introduced myself and briefly stated my job. The girl introduced herself as Susan. I confirmed that she had been at Bunscoill for her entire primary education, indicating that she was indeed a native speaker.

"Do you have any words in Manx you use around your friends that you wouldn't use around teachers?" Susan looked behind her to check that Paul was not nearby. She turned back and nodded. I paused for a second in surprise. "Really?" I asked. Susan nodded again.

"We have plenty. They aren't *bad* really, but we all know that Paul doesn't like us using fake words so we don't use them."

"So they aren't real words, you don't think?"

"Well, they aren't in our dictionaries. We all know what they mean though."

"How do you all know what they mean?"

"Usually they're English words mixed with a bit of Manx." Susan seemed quite happy to talk about the subject at this point.

"And do you make these words often?"

"Not *just* me. But yeah, whenever there isn't a word for something in Manx, we just take an English word and put all the Manx endings on it."

I couldn't contain my smile. This bit of information indicated that the children used Manx regularly enough to require a more complete vocabulary than its current lexicon could offer. Like any natural language, when a word doesn't exist, it is either borrowed or invented. The fact that the children "put the Manx endings" on their invented words indicates that there is a true loanword relationship between English and Manx, not a simple case of substitution. Indeed, Manx is more alive than the Bunscoill teachers may believe.

After I gave Julie a summary of my day at the school (including my discovery of Manx slang, which Julie was quite surprised to learn), I decided to ask her the question that had been weighing most heavily on my mind.

"As far as I can tell, Manx was more or less extinct by 1970," I began.

"I'd say so, yes."

"And it seems that it remained that way until the mid-90s, at least."

"More or less, yes."

"But here, a little more than ten years later, Manx has gone from five speakers to over fifty. That's a tenfold increase."

Julie laughed. "It is quite impressive, isn't it?"

Bunscoill children negotiate ownership of some yarn in Manx.

"So, how can you account for that change? What made people start caring about Manx all of a sudden? I mean—what made an island change its mind overnight?"

Julie took a sip of her tea. She set her cup down on the table, crossed her legs on the couch, and stared pensively into the hallway behind me. I heard children running and screaming, yelling back and forth at each other in Manx.

"I suppose people were fed up, really," Julie said.

"Fed up?"

"With the corruption, the laundering, the banking, all of that. It wore on us all. So much money and business flowing in from all over, and I suppose a lot of people felt that it was hard to be Manx anymore."

"How so?"

"A lot of people—well, certainly me and the people I knew—we were trying to figure out what it meant to be Manx. It didn't have to do with banking, we were quite sure of that. And what I found—what a lot of people found was this language that's been dormant in our culture. And it was time to bring it back."

I heard a child scream in some mix of Manx and unintelligible childspeak behind me. Julie cracked a slight smile.

"So that's how I'd account for it," she concluded.

FOURTEEN

The drill sergeant's orders woke me up again. More than a week into my stay, I still couldn't sleep through the morning drills. Chris seemed to manage: he was lying face down in his bed and snoring loudly.

I had spent the past week in Adrian's Manx lessons, sitting in on Adrian's classes for children (which, I learned, were an effective way to learn a language) and speaking with whomever I could pin down for a few minutes, carefully recording their Manx speech. I also spent a day in Ramsey, a town in the northern end of the Island, where I recorded a few locals speaking English for the Global Accent Database (an online collection of English accents worldwide). Any time I didn't spend learning or recording Manx I spent exploring the Island, discovering for myself what it had to offer.

This day was a bright Saturday. The sun sparkled on a glittering ocean, and the trees outside the dormitory rustled indignantly in the light breeze. I threw on my jacket and walked out to catch the morning bus.

I was due at Manx Radio's broadcasting headquarters in Douglas to meet with Adrian and a few of his friends. They were using one of the station's recording studios to dub over a popular British cartoon, *Friends and Heroes* (*Caarjyn as Gastaghyn* in Manx). Of the Island's three radio stations (Energy FM, 3 FM and Manx Radio), Manx Radio was the only station that agreed to lend its recording equipment to the group of Manx speakers.

The bus dropped me at the bay at Douglas's base. A few directions from helpful locals pointed me "just a short ways up" the steep hills that surround the town of Douglas. Fifteen minutes of trekking later, I came across a small office building with a radio antenna rising behind it like a gothic spire.

I rang the doorbell. Adrian came to greet me.

"Ah, hello! Hope you found the place alright?"

"Well, I had to do a bit of hiking, actually," I said.

"Yes, but it's worth it for the view, innit?" I was so focused on my destination that I had forgotten to examine my surroundings while I ascended the hill toward the radio station. I turned around and was stunned to see the town of Douglas far below. The town was calm in the mellow light of the early afternoon. The weekend seemed to cast its own sort of light on the Island; in Los Angeles, the streets are busy whether it be a weekday or a weekend, but in Douglas, the town's mood shifts as the week cycles, and this Saturday was a quiet one.

Adrian led me through a hallway, up a flight of stairs, and into a recording studio.

"This is the team," Adrian said. We were separated from the "team" by a slab of glass: inside the booth was Paul, who sat in front of a laptop with headphones dangling from around his neck. A blonde boy in a familiar blue sweater stood on a stool, looking upward toward a microphone.

"This is Ruben. He's one of Bunscoill's brightest," Adrian said with a smile. The setup was simple: Paul turned his laptop screen toward Ruben and, as the small boy's character talked on screen, Ruben would voice along the words. The process would repeat until the recording matched the movements of the character's lips nearly enough.

"Some of the dialog had to be changed a bit," Adrian explained. "Sometimes it takes a lot longer to say things in Manx than it does in English, so we had to cut a few of the lines down." Ruben spoke his lines with great gusto, acting out his character's motions atop his stool. Adrian grabbed a DVD sleeve from a nearby table and handed it to me.

The sleeve was identical to the original English version except for the words *Cargyn as Fagnyn* in place of the original title. The backside was an exact copy as well, but the English text had been replaced by a Manx translation.

"Paul thought that the presentation was important," Adrian explained. "A Bunscoill student sees two movies, one with a nice, professional English cover and one with an amateurish Manx one. Which one does the student buy? Better chances with the pretty cover, don't you think?" After a few more minutes of recording, Paul closed his laptop and stood up.

"*Feer vie, Ruben,*" Paul announced. Ruben smiled and hopped down from his stool. Paul saw me through the soundproof glass and nodded at me, and the pair walked out into the mixing room.

Adrian looked toward Paul. "Would you care to show Nick what we have so far, Paul?"

"Sure, why not?" Paul opened up his laptop on the mixing board and pressed the space bar.

The cartoon was like any other, really, except for the Manx dialog. The Manx speech fit the characters' mouth movements almost exactly, and the voice acting was quite professional.

"That's amazing," I said.

"I'll be honest, it took a long time to get it all to work," Paul said with a smile. On screen, an elderly man appeared.

"That's Brian's voice!" I said.

"Yeah, he was more than happy to help out, actually. He agrees that getting Manx-language media out there is important. Even if they're just translations right now, it's the first step to building culture. Don't you think, Adrian?" Adrian gave a proud smile.

Ruben, Paul and Adrian recording at Manx Radio.

* * *

The next item on my agenda was to track down a copy of the Manx bible. I decided to start my search at Rushen Abbey, the Liverpool students' excavation site. Chris told me that the students walked to the dig site every day, and I saw no reason why I shouldn't walk as well.

Rushen Abbey, a thirty-minute hike from Castle Rushen, sits in Ballasalla (*Balla Sallagh* in Manx, meaning "the willow tree village"). The abbey was founded in 1134 under the Scandinavian ruler King Olaf I for monks of the French Savignac order, a particularly strict order that mandated almost constant wakefulness for prayer. The abbey was completed in 1257 (over one hundred years after construction began). In the first half of the 16th century, Henry VIII dissolved all monastic communities under the Crown's authority, and Rushen Abbey was essentially left to decompose until the Manx National Heritage Organization (*Eiraght Ashoonagh Vannin* in Manx) adopted the site in 1998. Ten years later, a group of Liverpool students arrived to help excavate a structure that had just been discovered beneath the grassy surface of the Abbey green.

When I arrived at the excavation site, the early afternoon sun was shining brightly. A few clouds were scattered across the sky, and the freshly dug grass smelled sweet in the air. A large, fenced-off region stood in the middle of the Abbey's central courtyard, and a large, square trench sank deep beneath the surface. A maze of ancient, stone walls ran inside the trench.

Chris and Ellie chatted idly as they scraped dirt off of a stretch of wall. Rain was sitting in a corner, scribbling furiously in his journal.

"Hey Rain." I leaned over the edge of the trench. "How's the dig going?"

Rain kept his head buried in his moleskin. "It is going," he responded. A moment of silence ensued. A few birds chirped in the distance.

"So, who runs this dig?"

"His name is Ray." Rain continued scribbling. I craned my head over his shoulder.

"What are you drawing?"

Rain snapped his journal shut and looked me in the eye. "Perhaps you can find Ray in the tea room." Rain picked up his spade, placed a small blue hat over his head, and got back to work.

I walked across the grounds to a room in the abbey proper, facing the courtyard. A cramped chamber had apparently been converted into a sort of lounge, complete with teakettle and biscuits.

A tall man with long, blonde hair and a red beanie sat in a small, wooden chair reading the Guardian. He flipped his paper onto his lap and addressed me in a distinctly British accent. "Are you one of the Liverpool lot? Haven't seen you before."

"Oh, no—I'm an American actually." The man raised his eyebrows. "I'm actually here studying the Manx language, and I'm trying to collect

Manx-language books, and I thought this would be a good place to start to find the Manx bible."

The man's face cracked into a full smile. He rose from his seat and extended his hand. "Well, pleasure to meet you then. I'm Ray."

"Nick. Nice to meet you."

"So, a Manx bible, issit? Wait here a second. Make yourself some tea." Ray walked out of the room. I poured myself some boiling water and dropped a teabag in. Ten minutes later, Ray returned with a leather bound, purple book. On the front, the words "Manx Bible" were embossed in gold letters.

"So, what are you planning to do with this, exactly?" asked Ray, taking the seat across from me.

"Well, I thought it would make a nice present for my headmaster. He sponsored this trip, after all. But, I think it would be the first Manx Bible to make its way to North America."

"First out of Europe, probably."

"Really?"

"Wouldn't surprise me."

"Well, I'm actually trying to find as many Manx language books as I can. I don't think there's any Manx literature in the United States, and I'd like to start a collection."

"That sounds admirable. Where do you plan on finding these books, then?"

Rain at work at Rushen Abbey.

"Well—" I took a sip of tea to mask my thoughts. After I gulped the sip down, I still hadn't thought of an answer. "I'm not sure, really. Do you have any ideas?"

"Well, I have a few..." Ray took out a notebook and began writing. "Some of these people will have Manx books, some will know people who have Manx books. Either way, a lead's a lead, innit?" Ray ripped the page out from his journal and handed it to me. It was a list of names and shops with their respective villages. "The good news is, there isn't much written down in Manx to begin with, so I guess you won't have to find a whole lot. Right?"

I folded the paper and slipped into my messenger bag. "I guess not."

* * *

I spent the rest of my day hunting. I took the bus from village to village: Peel to Port Erin to Ramsey to Kirk Michael to Douglas to Port Ayre. I stopped in a village, talked to the shopkeep Ray had recommended, bought whatever books they had, and took whatever leads they gave me. Seven hours later, I ran out of new names, and I caught the last bus home to Castletown. At either side, I had two shopping bags filled with all sixteen books written in the Manx language.

I returned to King William's long after everyone had gone to bed. I crept through the hallways of the dorm as I kept my two shopping bags filled with books firmly at my sides. I set one down to creak open the door, and I snuck quickly into my bed.

Since its first airing in 1964, Manx Radio has played an announcement before shutting down each night:

"To those of you who guard and protect us during the night, to the police and firemen, to those in the lighthouse service and the coastguards, to doctors and nurses attending the sick, indeed to all who have to work while others sleep, we wish a quiet and peaceful night.

"To the fisherman at sea, and to all those who earn their living on the great waters around our little Island, fair winds and good sailing.

"From all of us at Manx Radio, the voice of Man, goodnight."

A few trees rustled outside. Somewhere far away, a cargo boat sounded its foghorn. The last plane of the day had already landed at the airport, and the only illumination in the night was the twinkling stars and the crescent moon that shone through the window. The moonlight painted a quiet silver across the room. I closed my eyes, rolled over, and drifted gently away.

FIFTEEN

After Reverend John Kelly (author of the original Manx Grammar) finished his translation of the Bible into Manx, he was asked to bring his completed manuscript to Whitehaven, Cumbria so it could be printed en masse. Rev. Kelly was shipwrecked in a storm on his way from Douglas and, floating alone in the middle of the turbulent Irish Sea, he held his translation of the Bible above his head for five hours until he was rescued, assuring that the manuscript would not be damaged by the water.

Rev. Kelly obviously understood the importance of literature in culture. Kelly's main objective was to enlighten the Manx people by allowing them to interpret the Bible for themselves. Not only did he achieve his objective wonderfully, Kelly left behind a shining example of the effect of mass media on culture.

Today, referring to a book as "mass media" seems laughable. However, when Kelly published his Bible in the latter half of the 18th century, the book became a common household item on the Island. One rural woman who could neither speak nor read English proclaimed after reading the Manx Bible, "Until today, I have lived my life in darkness. I have been blind, but today I can see." Most Manx people had never interpreted the Bible for themselves. It had been interpreted for them by British preachers who spoke Manx or Manx preachers who spoke English. For the first time, a Manxman didn't have to learn English to discover the Bible for himself.

Although the publication of a Manx-language Bible may appear as little more than a heart-warming piece of history, the story illustrates a crucial point about the relationship between language and media. Although the Manx Bible was hugely significant in its time, today it has drifted into obscurity. Ultimately, few other books were translated into Manx. In fact, little media was produced in Manx at all, and the social stigma carried by the Manx language caused the majority of educated Manxmen to write in English. When Professor Carl Marstrander asked Joseph Woodworth why he hadn't used Manx in so many years, Woodworth replied, "Everything worth reading is in English, isn't it?"

Today, most television programs in the Isle of Man are British or American. Although many British movies are shot on the Isle of Man due to its relaxed regulations and tax-haven status, few films are made with Manx actors and Manx production companies, and there are certainly no Manx-language movies. As Jennifer of *Bunscoill* pointed out, the market for such a movie would simply be too small. The songs played on the Island's radio stations are overwhelmingly British and American, and only a few of the

television stations broadcasting on the Island bother to hire Manx reporters for local news. The mass media of the Isle of Man are, essentially, imported goods.

So what were Adrian and his friends getting at with their Manx dub of *Friends and Heroes*? The project serves to entertain the relatively small demographic of Manx-speaking children (that is, the forty-or-so Bunscoill students); however, these students are all native English speakers as well, and would be just as likely to enjoy the original, English voice acting. There is, of course, a larger purpose to the project: to create a work of authentic Manx output. Yes, the cartoon will be a work in translation, of course, but it will not be a matter of repackaging and remarketing, or a matter of loading a shipment onto a ferry and converting the price from British pounds to Manx pounds. The finished work will be a product of Manx hands. A product with a cover as professional as any slick, London-designed DVD sleeve. It will show the Island that media doesn't only come from global superpowers.

One question remains: to what extent does self-produced media fortify a language's use within a culture? It is difficult to reach to history for examples; as Cormac McCarthy wrote in *All the Pretty Horses*, "there are no control groups in history"—that is, it is impossible to discern what may have occurred in the absence of one factor or another. However, we may

examine a few recently extinct languages to gain a rough idea about the
topic: Akkala Sami (Russia, extinct 2003), Atsugewi (California, 1988),
Kakadu (Australia, 2002), Munichi (Peru, 1996), Ubykh (Turkey, 1992).
All of these languages had a very small population of speakers before their
death, and all of them produced no media whatsoever. After the speaker
count fell under 1,000, no literature was written in these languages. No
popular music was written, no films were shot, and no plays were put on in
these languages. Languages with a relatively low number of speakers (such
as Welsh, Breton, Irish Gaelic, Basque, Catalan and Cornish) have avoided
complete extinction through a large effort to preserve the language's use
through an output of original music, dance and (in the case of Scottish
Gaelic) film in the language. To use Manx as an example, Isle of Man hosts
the yearly *Yn Cruinnacht* festival, an inter-Celtic festival in which
musicians and artists speak and perform in minority Celtic languages
(Manx, Breton, Welsh, Irish Gaelic, Scottish Gaelic and Cornish).
Ultimately, when a culture ceases to produce its own art, its unique identity
often whithers away, as well. As Julie Matthews of Bunscoill said, there was
a period during which many people forgot "what it meant to be Manx."

We will never know exactly what motivated John Kelly to hold his
translation of the Bible above his head for five hours while floating in the
sea. As a reverend, he was probably more concerned with the fate of the
Manx people's souls than the fate of the Manx people's language. However,
his work ultimately reached outside of the spiritual realm, helping to
illustrate a crucial point of language endangerment and extinction: media
matters.

A Breton band plays at *Yn Cruinnacht*.

Sixteen

There were three reasons why I was surprised to win a fellowship from my school. The first reason, of course, was the utterly obscure nature of the project's goal and subject matter. The second, however, was that I confessed that I expected to make no real difference in our world. I did not expect to restore Manx to its former glory, or even to teach the language to a single non-speaker, aside from myself. My goal was simply to ask "why?" Why did Manx become extinct, and why did it come back to life? The third reason was that I confessed that I found Manx relatively unimportant on its own. As intriguing and mysterious as the language's history is (not to mention the Island itself), the story of Manx has little consequence to humanity as a whole. It is the larger phenomenon that Manx's story reflects that makes the story of Manx useful.

Until very recently, the Island was a place where a single people lived in relative isolation from the rest of the world. It was a place where all factors could be accounted for clearly and precisely. The insular case of the Manx language, I imagined, would allow me to make broader conclusions about the new and frighteningly little-known issue of language extinction.

There is a single, overarching question on the subject: why does any language become extinct? Why are more languages going extinct today than at any time in history? Languages are not like animals; we cannot blame such changes on fossil fuels or overfishing or clear-cutting the rainforest.

Indeed, Manx does teach us a few important lessons about language death. Ultimately, speaking English evolved into a crucial skill as it became necessary for Manx people to trade and interact with English speakers. A market of potential clients and customers spoke English and, from shipping to tourism to offshore banking, English was simply good for business. From this point onward, Manx became associated with a lower social class, and this social stigma discouraged parents from teaching their children Manx. Due to a low level of education before English influence and a low desire to become educated in Manx after English influence, little literature, art or music was produced in Manx, and the Manx-language art that does exist is mostly comprised of folk tales and folk music. Thus, the language became moribund, and was effectively replaced by the English language.

Many languages have followed a story roughly similar to that of Manx. The Ös language of Turkey, for example, is now almost completely moribund; it has been pushed to an extremely endangered status as most of its speakers chose to learn Turkish throughout much of the 20th century, and these native Ös speakers usually chose not to teach Ös to their children.

Fewer than 5,000 people (all of whom live in a single village in Rivers State) speak the Baan language of Nigeria. British linguists Oliver Bond and Greg Anderson portray a story similar to that of Manx in their study of the Baan language: "among the Eleme, this language is considered a mere 'dialect' and not worthy of study in its own right. This kind of negative local attitude to a language is instrumental in determining its status as an endangered language, as negative stigma associated with a particular speech variety usually lead to its use being associated with a lack of socio-economic power and mobility, furthering its eroding within its own community (parents choose not to teach their ancestral language to their children since they believe it will cause their children problems economically)."

In 1855, social and economic forces similar to those experienced by Manx speakers forced twenty-seven tribes of Siletz Indians in Oregon (all of whom had different languages) to surrender their tribal tongues and both learn English and agree upon a single lingua franca, Chinuk Jargon. Today, only one of the original languages of the Siletz tribes remains. The language, Siletz Dee-ni, has only one living speaker.

The list goes on. Todzhu, Dukha, Tsengel, Monchak, Tofa, Cayuse, Chemakum, Eyak, Molala, Pánobo (to name only a few) have all disappeared from the face of the earth. Larger, more widely spoken languages have replaced all of these tongues, usually for a mix of the same economic and social reasons that contributed to Manx's rapid decline.

In an era of instant, global communication, in which one human being can be in near-constant contact with any other human being regardless of geography, it is not difficult to imagine why maintaining a minority language in the face of a larger, more global language is not in many cultures' best economic interests. A global language such as English, French or Chinese can open a culture up to new markets and new ideas.

This phenomenon of a global, widely spoken language influencing a culture with a less internationally spoken language exists outside of language extinction and endangerment. Today, English is the *lingua franca* of science, business, technology and medicine; it is currently the most-taught second language in the world, and it enjoys the unique privilege of exporting the greatest number of loanwords worldwide. From the over 200 English words used in everyday Japanese to verbs such as *googlear* (to google") and *hacer windsurfing* in Spanish, the reach of the English language is truly global. English is often absorbed into other languages: for example German speakers make their own compound nouns from English words (such as *Softwareversion* from the English "software version") and Japanese speakers often create brand new words (called *wasei-eigo,* or "made-in-Japan English") from English loanwords (such as *pasokon,* which combines the English words "personal" and "computer" in a way that no native English speaker would think to do). This influence exists in the world of pop culture, as well: Sweden, for example, has exported a large amount of popular music in the past 30 years, most of it in English. The popularity of

English-language media worldwide inspired the ratification of the "Touban Laws" of France, which assure that all advertisements must contain a French translation of foreign words, and that at least 40% of all songs on the radio must be in French. Through this process, which is jokingly referred to as Americanization (or, more pejoratively, "Cocacolanization"), the English language has found its way into many powerful, global languages such as German and French, not to mention into languages backed by less economically powerful countries.

To put the urgency of language extinction in perspective, we may compare the phenomenon with the extremely well publicized issue of animal extinction. As of 2008, 8% of all plants and 18% of all animals, including 5% of fishes and 11% of birds, are endangered. As of 2008, over 40% of all living tongues are endangered. As mentioned earlier, 52% of the world's languages are spoken by less than 10,000 people, and 83% of languages are confined to a single country. Although language death is nothing new, what is new is the fact that no languages are rising to take the places of these fallen languages; previously, a language would die after it had evolved into a new language through cultural interaction or simply due to the passage of time. Today, however, a dead language is not replaced with a brand new one, but instead replaced with a more-powerful, already-existing language. In fact, only nine languages have managed to exert this sort of influence outside of their native cultures: Mandarin Chinese, Hindustani, Spanish, Arabic, Russian, French, Portuguese, German and, perhaps above all, English. Six of these nine languages are European, and even native speakers of these languages are beginning to learn English as a second language.

One part of Manx's story is left unexamined in the context of the larger world: its revival. Manx was essentially brought back from the dead for reasons that are difficult to isolate. Most likely, the loss of a distinct Manx identity attributed to its boom in popularity (most notably the founding of *Bunscoill*).

This revival is not a unique event. Regarding the Ös language of Turkey, a group of its few remaining speakers are only now writing the first book ever to be published in the Ös language, and Dr. Gregory D. S. Anderson and Dr. K. David Harrison from the Hans Rausing Endangered Language Program are currently in the process of documenting the language and spreading awareness and interest in the tongue to the younger generation.

Living Tongues Institute For Endangered Languages has launched a full program to teach the dying Baan language of Nigeria to locals, hoping to assure that English does not push out the language completely.

The Living Tongues Institute also helped the last speaker of Siletz Dee-ni, Bud Lane, compile an online talking dictionary with 988 words of the language. Bud Lane has been working tirelessly since 2003 to revitalize the language among his tribe members, and regularly teaches classes on the endangered language (much like Brian and Adrian do with Manx.)

Other Celtic languages like Welsh, Irish Gaelic, Cornish and Breton have all been rescued from almost certain eradication by a fairly recent revival of interest among their respective ethnic groups.

It is entirely possible that Manx has exemplified a larger model of language extinction: decreased language use, imposition of a more global language upon a less global language, and revival of the endangered tongue. However, there are many exceptions to the this model; after all, about 10 languages have gone extinct every year since 1990.

At the end of the day, what has Manx taught us? Manx's story is not entirely a happy one, after all: although it has been saved from the brink of extinction, it is highly improbable that Manx will ever overtake English as the main language of the Isle of Man. Now that the Island's economy is closely linked to the world of banking and international investment, a workforce of native English speakers is one of the Island's most valuable assets, and this is unlikely to change.

Above all, the history of the Manx language has not given us a romantic picture of the future. It has provided us with a firmer, more tangible grasp of an issue that was formerly shrouded in mystery. It has provided a precedent for the stories of the endangered languages of the future. Manx has shown us how and why a language lies down to die, and how and why it may rise to live among us once again.

SEVENTEEN

Tucked into the row of shops that lines the winding, cobblestone streets of Peel was a small shop marked by a hand painted sign: "ARTS & ANTIQUES: BOUGHT, SOLD & TRADED. FREEMASONRY, BOOKS, ET CETERA."

The shop was stacked to the ceiling with shiny brass and deep, wooden brown. Stacks of books created a maze in the tiny room, and the smell of polished wood penetrated every corner of the shop.

"Hello young man." I whipped my head around. Behind me, a middle-aged woman with frizzy, brown hair and thin-rimmed glasses stood behind me, her neck craned forward.

"Oh, hello. I was just looking around, actually—"

"Oh, well listen to your accent! Where are you from? America? Canada?"

I sighed to myself. "America."

"Well you aren't British and you aren't Irish, I know that. So what brings you all the way to our island?"

"I'm studying the Manx language, actually. Oh, you know, as long as I'm here... Do you have any books in Manx?"

"Books in Manx?" The woman smiled. "No, young man, I'm afraid I don't. 'Tis a bit hard to find books in Manx, you know."

"So I'm gathering," I said with a smile.

"Well, there must be something I can help you with. How long are you here for?"

"I've been here for about two and a half weeks. I'm leaving tomorrow, actually."

"Have you anything to remember the Island by?"

"Well, I have the books I've collected in Manx, I have pictures—"

"Yes, but something to *really* remember it by?" I stared dumbly at her. Her expression was an unwavering sort of understanding and, after a moment, she turned and walked behind a bookshelf. "Just a minute, then."

A few moments later, the woman emerged with a small, black box. She made her way over to me and pushed the box into my hand.

"Go on, open it," she said. Inside the box was a small, silver necklace. A thin chain hooked around a familiar symbol: three legs, joined at the center inside of a circle. The silver was scratched, and the chain had a distinct age to it. "Do you recognize this symbol?" the woman asked.

"Yes, it's the triskelion." The symbol decorates the Manx flag, and it appears quite often throughout the Island.

"Very good," the woman said with a smile. "And do you know what it means?"

"Well... Not exactly."

"The motto of the Island is Quocunque Jeceris Stabit. Do you know any Latin? You're studying a language, surely you should know some Latin."

It had been a few years since I'd studied Latin. I strained to remember Ms. Price's lessons. "Wherever... you throw it, it will stand?"

"Exactly." The woman gave a broader smile. "Do you see what the symbol means now?" I looked down at the symbol. I stared into the perpendicular angles of the legs' joints, the details of the silver, the lines etched into the metal. I flipped the necklace over. On the backside, it said "MANX SILVER."

"This one's quite special. Handcrafted from Port Erin's silver. The jeweler who made these, before he gave them to me, he said to not show them to just anyone. But something brought you here all the way here from the United States, isn't it?" I nodded. "You were thrown here, and you stood, didn't you?" I thought for a moment, then nodded hesitantly. "Turn around, then," she concluded. The woman took the necklace from the box and clipped it around my neck. "Now, hide that under your clothes and remember it when you need it. You'll do that, won't you?"

Once again at a loss for words, I simply nodded. The woman began to walk away. "Wait! How much do I owe you?" I called after her.

"Oh, don't you worry about it. It'll make a good story for your American friends." The woman disappeared behind a stack of books.

I felt the necklace under my sweater as I rode the bus to Douglas, a hard circle against my ribcage. I was meeting Adrian and Brian one last time before I left, hoping to sum up my findings on the Island.

One twenty-minute bus ride and one twenty-minute walk later, I arrived in front of 18 Hillary Road once again. A darker gray was breaking through a lighter one as the afternoon began to settle behind the sea. I knocked on the door. Adrian answered, smiling broadly.

"Come in, come in!" I walked into Brian's study. Brian threw his arms in the air and smiled. "Hooray! I just finished boiling the water, too. Is peppermint alright?" Brain asked, gesturing toward his tea kettle.

We sat down. Adrian told us about his latest lesson at an elementary school in Ramsey in which the children were particularly receptive to Manx. Brian told us about an essay he was writing concerning Manx place names throughout the ages, and about a conversation he had with a former colleague from his past life as a physicist. I told them about my work, my book collection, my progress with Manx, and my experience

The antique shop in Peel.

with the children in Bunscoill. We told stories and laughed as the sky outside darkened.

"Well, I'm glad we've been helpful to you, Nick," Brian said.

"You've been more than helpful! Do you know how much Manx I learned in only the past few weeks?"

Brian laughed. "Yes, I remember how it was with Ned Maddrell and me."

"He taught you Manx, didn't he?"

"That's right," Brian said. He picked up his teacup, preparing to take a sip. "I'd follow him all around, wherever he went, and I'd point to things and ask him what they were called in Manx. And I'd keep up conversation as much as I could. Must have annoyed him quite a bit, the poor man. Awfully nice of him, though... An old man teaching a young kid like me." The vigor behind Brian's broad grin disappeared suddenly, and the expression that remained was a strange, empty trace of a smile long forgotten. Brian took a slow sip of tea. "Well, young at the time, you know," he concluded softly.

A silence swept across Brian's face. He set his teacup down on the table with a soft clink. He turned his head to the window, and a dark shade fell over his white beard. Brian stared off through the glass into the fleeting light of the day's remainder, his blue eyes fixed upon something I could not see. He stared unblinkingly into the street with a mix of satisfaction and resignation, the face of a parent whose child has just moved out to start a new life in a far-away town.

Adrian furrowed his brow and followed Brian's gaze outward. After a few moments of searching the street aimlessly, his focus drifted back toward Brian. His eyebrows relaxed. He understood, though indirectly. Adrian lifted his sleeve up to check his watch, then leaned back and looked toward me.

I looked out the window too. The night was rushing into the port town. A clerk was closing up his shop across the street. A few seagulls floated above the buildings, traveling inland. A man in a smart-looking suit walked by, returning home after a day of work in one bank or another. My eyes flickered back toward Brian. Brian's focus had softened. The corners of his mouth had turned upward almost undetectably.

"*Feer vie*," Brian said.

"*Feer vie*," I answered.

EIGHTEEN

The word "tradition" comes from the Latin *traditionem*, which literally means "handing down." Language is like all traditions: it is passed from generation to generation and, when one generation fails to teach a tradition to the next, the tradition begins to die.

Language is, however, the most peculiar of all traditions: every culture has one, and all languages are at once disparate and similar. Every culture on earth has invented its own language and, using wildly different grammars and sounds, every one can plant the same images, concepts and ideas in the minds of its listeners. Linguists such as Noam Chomsky and Steven Pinker speculate that language is a deep instinct, common to all human beings. Even as early as the turn of the 19th century, American lexicographer Noah Webster proclaimed that "language is not an abstract construction of the learned, or of dictionary makers, but is something arising out of the work, needs, ties, joys, affections, tastes, of long generations of humanity, and has its bases broad and low, close to the ground."

Although our common use of language is a uniting factor, our linguistic diversity also highlights the diversity of our human perceptions. Ranka Bjeljac-Babic, lecturer at the University of Poitiers (France), comments on this diversity:

"To grasp how differently each tongue reflects the world, one only needs to list the words that crop up in every language with exactly the same meaning. Words like I, you, us, who, what, no, all, one, two, big, long, small, woman, man, eat, see, hear, sun, moon, star, water, fire, hot, cold, white, black, night, land. There are about 300 at the most."

The question I hear most often when I explain my project to others (after they have asked me why Manx is important, and after I have explained that its story is important primarily as a tool to understand language extinction) is: "why should we care about language extinction?" It is true, after all, that fewer world languages would facilitate global communication. Fewer languages would lead to a better understanding between peoples and, perhaps, a decrease in prejudice. Indeed, the spread of global languages is not without benefit.

Bejeljac-Babic gives a wonderful explanation of the benefits of linguistic diversity:

"It is possible that if we all ended up speaking the same language, our brains would lose some of their natural capacity for linguistic inventiveness. We would never be able to plumb the origins of human language or resolve the mystery of 'the first language.' As each language dies, a chapter of human history closes. Multilingualism is the most accurate reflection of multiculturalism. The destruction of the first will inevitably lead to the loss of the second. Imposing a language without any links to a people's culture and way of life stifles the expression of their collective genius. A language is not only the main instrument of human communication. It also expresses the world vision of those who speak it, their imagination and their ways of using knowledge."

If we no longer possess the full range of human language, we cease to understand the full range of our species. When we lose the many voices of man, we lose sight of what a human being can be.

Language death is not a black-and-white issue, of course. There are benefits and drawbacks to decreased linguistic diversity. It is, however, a phenomenon that must be understood. So far, the rapid pace of language death and the alarming decrease in linguistic (and cultural) diversity worldwide has been noticed by few and understood by fewer. Our languages—indeed, the face of our species—is changing. We are becoming closer together. Our world is becoming smaller. If the global forces at work behind language death continue on, we will wake up one day in a world much different from the one we live in now.

As far as the Isle of Man itself goes, the Island has kept good on its promise: wherever it has been thrown, it has stood. The Island has adapted to new rules, new governments and new industries with amazing ease, and, though small, the Island soldiers on. The triskelions that decorate the Island serve as constant reminders for the citizens of Man. The symbol represents what has come to pass and what is yet to come. Although the Manx language suffered a few years of true death, it is abundantly clear to me that the Island is a place where nothing truly dies.

NINETEEN

I woke up early without the help of the drill sergeant that morning. My phone's alarm buzzed me awake under my pillow. The world was the same dark blue as it was when I arrived. A few leaves rustled. Far away, a train whistle blew. Rain and Chris were fast asleep in their beds. I had said my goodbyes the night before, so I took my already-packed bags and rolled them out into the street.

The wind bit at me, even as I huddled under my overcoat. The airport was a fifteen minute walk from the King William's grounds, and I decided I'd rather get up fifteen minutes earlier than travel idly in a cab. After all, I had sixteen hours of idle travel ahead of me.

I walked past barley fields, a few plots divided by stone walls where sheep and cows slept. While I walked, I imagined what I would tell my friends about my trip. About Brian, about the tower in Port Erin, about the woman in the antique shop. How I would explain Manx's story to them, or how I would explain language death in general. I imagined writing a book about what I had found. I laughed. Nobody would read a book about Manx, I thought.

I waited for an hour or so in the terminal, sipping on tea and watching a few cars rush past the road outside. My flight was called through the loudspeaker, and I was escorted out of the terminal and into the runway.

Far off in the distance, obscured in a blue haze like some Renaissance painting, the blue-faced clock tower of King William's stood like a giant watching over the farmland. The clock face showed 5:00, and I imagined the sound of the bells sweeping through the college ground, crashing into Chris' and Rain's ears as they awoke. I was pointed into the same propeller plane that took me there.

Sitting in the plane, it felt as if I had traveled sixteen hours from Los Angeles and dreamed the strangest dream. A waking dream in which I visited a curious, northern island, learned a curious language, and met many curious people. I felt as if I had just awoken, and I was now boarding the same plane I had arrived in and was heading back toward Los Angeles. The plane's propellers began to rumble and, after a burst of acceleration, we set off.

Drifting upward, parting from the land, a curious northern island shrank beneath me. Just over the horizon the sun began to rise, and the sea and its Island sparkled brilliantly in the youth of a new day.

ABOUT THE AUTHOR

Nick Merrill was born on the Halloween of 1990. He is currently a senior at the Harvard-Westlake School in Los Angeles, California, and plans to pursue a career in academia (read: socially-acceptable unemployment) studying language and linguistics. The Voice of Man is Nick's first published work, and (he hopes) far from his last.

Besides Manx, Nick speaks Japanese and Argentine Spanish (which he believes to be the finest flavor of the language). He is somewhat tone deaf, but does not let his disability prevent him from enjoying the sound of his banjo. Nick continues to wear the triskelion necklace (chapter seventeen) around his neck at all times as a reminder to always stand where he is thrown.

SOURCES CONSULTED

Basnett, Douglas. Premier Guide to the Isle of Man. Douglas, Isle of Man: Lily Publications, 2000.

Baxter, William. Manx written and spoken: A description of the grammar of the Manx Language with words and phrases from native speakers plus symbolised pronunciations of ... of Celtic languages useful but not essential. Douglas, Isle of Man: 'Y Graig', 1994.

Bird, Hinton. Island That Led: History of Manx Education. Port St. Mary, Isle of Man: Self-published, 1991.

Cregeen, Archibald. Cregeen's Manx dictionary. Montgomery: Brown, 1910.

Dearden, Steven, and Ken Hassell. Inner Mann. Douglas, Isle of Man: Stenlake Publishing, 2003.

Douglas, Andrew. Isle of Man: Then and now--a photographic journey. Lancaster: Celt Investments, 1996.

Gregor, Douglas Bartlett. Celtic: A Comparative Study of the Six Celtic Languages, Irish, Gaelic, Manx, Welsh, Cornish, Breton Seen Against the Background of Their History, Literature and Destiny. Cambridge: Oleander Press, 1980.

Hardy, Clive. Francis Frith's Isle of Man (Photographic Memories). Douglas, Isle of Man: Frith Book Company Ltd., 2005.

Kermode, David G.. Offshore Island Politics: The Constitutional and

Political Development of the Isle of Man in the Twentieth Century (Liverpool University Press - Centre for Manx Studies Monographs). Liverpool: Liverpool University Press, 2001.

Kinvig, R.H.. Isle of Man. Liverpool: Liverpool University Press, 1975.

Kniveton, Gordon N. A Chronicle of the 20th Century Volume 1 1901-1950 . Douglas, Isle of Man: Manx Experience , 1999.

Moore, Arthur William. The Story of the Isle of Man. Charleston, SC: Bibliobazaar, 2008.

Quilliam, Leslie. Surnames of the Manx. Castletown, Isle of Man: Cashtal Books, 1989.

Studies, Center For Manx. Practical Manx. Liverpool: Liverpool University Press, 2008.

Winterbottom, Derek. Governors of the Isle of Man. Grand Rapids: Manx Heritage Foundation, 1999.

100 years of heritage: The work of the Manx Museum and National Trust. Grand Rapids: Manx Museum And National Trust, 1986.

Excavations on St Patrick's Isle, Isle of Man, 1989-1992:: Prehistoric, Viking, Medieval And Later (Liverpool University Press - Centre for Manx Studies Monographs). Liverpool: Liverpool University Press, 2002.

Manx Ballads and Music (Celtic Language and Literature : Goidelic and Brythonic). New York: Ams Pr Inc, 1996.

www.ingramcontent.com/pod-product-compliance
Lightning Source LLC
Chambersburg PA
CBHW032137040426
42449CB00005B/287